Paper Words

Paper Words

Discovering and Living with My Autism

Judy Endow, MSW

Foreword by Fred R. Volkmar, MD

© 2009 Autism Asperger Publishing Co.
P.O. Box 23173
Shawnee Mission, Kansas 66283-0173
www.asperger.net

Publisher's Cataloging-in-Publication

Endow, Judy.
    Paper words : discovering and living with my autism / Judy Endow, MSW; foreword by Fred Volkmar. -- 1st ed. -- Shawnee Mission, KS : Autism Asperger Pub. Co., 2009.

       p. ; cm.
       ISBN: 978-1-934575-49-9
       LCCN: 2009927797

       Summary: Through free verse, we follow the author's journey toward understanding her "differentness". In the process, we learn how her mind works and how she tries to cope and deal with her differences in everyday life.

       1. Endow, Judy. 2. Autism. 3. Developmentally disabled-- Biography. 4. People with mental disabilities--Biography. 5. Selfreliant living. I. Volkmar, Fred. II. Title.

RC553.A88 E53 2009   2009927797
616.85882--dc22   0905

This book is designed in Helvetica Neue.

Printed in the United States of America.

In the Springtime of youth
    little boys
        love
           their mamas   big

              with   wonder.

In the Summertime of youth
    teenage boys
        love
           their mamas   big

              with   questions.

During the Fall of youth
    young men
        love
           their mamas   big

              with   distance.

In the Winter,   when youth is put to sleep,
    adult sons
        love
           their mamas   big

              with   budding understanding

        To David, Paul and Daniel –

           hoping that
           you'll always know

                your mama's   love
                transcends all   your seasons.

Table of Contents

FOREWORD

Autism was first described in 1943 by Leo Kanner as a disorder of "affective contact." Kanner speculated that individuals with autism grew up outside the usual "world of people." In the decades subsequent to his work, our conception of autism and related autism spectrum conditions has changed significantly, but Kanner's key insight into the social difficulties that characterize autism has remained.

Research has clarified that the early lack of social engagement makes for major differences in a range of other areas – attention, perception, cognition, and communication. Research has also made it clear that there is a broader range of the condition than was first believed. As we have come to better understand some of these differences, we have become able to think about new ways of accommodating the needs of individuals with autism and related conditions. Thankfully, the move to earlier and more sustained interventions has made it possible for more and more individuals on the autism spectrum to achieve adult independence and self-sufficiency.

While much of our knowledge about autism and related disorders has come from research, much of our understanding of the experience of autism has come from parents, siblings, and, increasingly, persons with autism spectrum disorders who write and speak about their own experiences. These efforts enrich our understanding of autism as they come from the unique vantage point of personal experience of the condition.

In *Paper Words*, Judy Endow provides a unique and moving account of her experience. Through her story and poetry, she presents her life story in a way that helps us understand her feelings and responses in dealing with an often confusing and perplexing world. The construction of her narrative allows us to appreciate the complexities of understanding and coping with the world in a way most of us can't experience. This volume will be of great interest to parents, teachers, and researchers. It reminds us of the importance of listening to individuals with autism and related conditions and their unique ways of experiencing and coping with the world.

Fred R. Volkmar, MD
Director, Child Study Center
Irving B. Harris Professor of Child Psychiatry, Pediatrics and Psychology
Yale University

INTRODUCTION

Paper words
    can be heard;
        so speak up, ink,
           and say them!

       Speaking words
           are burdensome;
              they get her
                  lost   and tangled,

              So,   pen and ink
                  are her first choice
                    to voice
                        what she's not saying.

When speaking   words,
    two people should
        take their turns
           to say them.

       Start words   now,
              then stop   and wait,
                  then listen   some:
                    adds up to conversation.

But,   starting words
    and   stopping them;
        then,   hearing words
           and   seeing faces

      is much   too much
           to keep track   of
              when having
                conversation.

So,   paper words
    are much preferred,
        speak up, ink;
           now say them!

       Listen, people,
          to the ink;
              you won't get
                lost or   tangled!

*From Endow, J. (2006). *Making Lemonade: Hints for Autism's Helpers* (p. 96). Cambridge, WI: Cambridge Book Review Press. Reprinted with permission.

... and thus, using paper words, I set out to write this book. The purpose is to allow you to walk along with me through much of my life journey as my differences unfold, and as I ultimately discover my autism. Along the way, years before I was to ever have the label of autism applied to me, while an institutionalized teenager, I discovered my neurology. Of course, at that time, I was unaware that the word "neurology" described my discovery. In practical terms, I simply became able to see my insides in a new way.

Years later, as an adult – and still before I was diagnosed with autism – I collected little stones so that I could show a therapist how my insides looked to me. At that time, the label the therapist chose to apply to my inside reality was multiple personality disorder.

Today, I keep my collection of little stones in a tiny, clear plastic box that has a miniature toy magnifying glass imbedded in the cover. By now, I have come to know that the numerous tiny stones that make up my collection show a concrete replication of how the neurology of autism looks in my brain and subsequently plays out in my body. And because self-knowledge is not limited by the timeline of man's scientific discoveries, I was not only able to "see" my inside neurology decades ago, I was also able to begin developing strategies that allowed me to cope with my life as a person inside of a body headed up by the neurology of autism.

Today we understand autism so much better, and even so, our understanding is miniscule. We have so much more to discover and learn. When I hold my little plastic box of tiny stones, I can look at them and know they are tangible evidence that there is hope that the science of man will one day catch up to the experience of autism.

... and in the meantime,
        until then,

            I humbly invite you,
                    if you so wish,

            to come along
                    with me

                on this life long journey
                        of discovery ...

                ... a little plastic box of stones,
                        science,
                        God,

                        and for you,
                        Paper Words.

All my thoughts are in pictures. The words are a translation of the pictures I use when thinking. The spaces between letters and words represent how long it takes for the pictures to fluidly move in such a manner as to connect smoothly with the next thought. Many times when the looks of the words are changed, I totally lose the picture. When this happens, there is no picture to translate, and hence no words. It seems sort of crazy that changing spacing can be the same as completely deleting a poem, but it is so! I don't always like this, as in some cases I would rather have the words come more closely together so as to look more like traditional writing, but I have not been able to legislate this internally.

As mentioned later in this book, often when I have needed to figure out something in life, I write a poem. It helps when I can use my literal and concrete way of understanding the world to write about my everyday experiences.

CHAPTER ONE

DISCOVERING

MY

INSIDE WIRING

the unconnected

inside parts

of me

ushered forth

into

my awareness

… a concrete picture of my neurology

The Big Bang Prologue of Starting Over

When I was a teenager, the "too much" of life caught up with me. Everything in the world around me was just too much.

... too much noise with the varying sounds of the world clamoring to grab my attention, their pitches and tones wildly crashing into each other as if competing for a speed prize on a race track – or so I wished ... If only the cacophony of the world outside my skin would at least line up and compete in some orderly fashion – like race cars on a race track – it would then allow me to watch the color of each sound going around and around, and thus enable me to keep track of this forever multi-tonal, warped schizophrenic sound in the world all around me –

sounds   wildly speeding
  and crashing into each other
    polluting the air waves with
     nonsensical meaning able only
     to be   sorted out by retreating ...

   So ...

   I gathered up the stuff of me
    so that together we

   left that chaotic race track
    of the haphazard noises
     of human events
    never-endingly spewing forth
     entangling themselves
      hopelessly into
       each other

  spilling into eons of all eternity
    ready to   engulf
     my very being
    into their cumulative affect
     of the
      All of
       Everything

but   just in time
         I stopped   the world outside of
              my skin   from
                    its attempted   consumption

                         by mathematical   negation
                         through internal   realization

                    that the All   of Everything

               in the world   all around me
                    could be   easily
                         negated
                    by the None   of Nothing
                                   inside me.

               So I wiped   the slate clean
                    and started   again
                         using a personal   application
                    of the   Big Bang equation

                         reducing myself back   to
                              the None   of Nothing

and then   began
     moving carefully   forward

          little by little sorting out the
               world of   me

                    while simultaneously engaging in   a sensible
                         mathematically   progressive manner

               with the   space
                    outside of   me
                         on the other side
                    of my skin   where all of
                         the rest of   the world
                              happened,

          In that unending   big space
               where untold   numbers of
                    world-people talked and resided

10

... this Big Bang rebirthing   able to be
                ushered forth using the concepts of

                        mathematical division

                                    and

                        scientific metamorphosis.

I began   by dividing out
        the substance of   me
                from everything   else

        able to be accomplished by   the discovery
                that the   concept of division

                could be transformed into   personal reality
                        by using   my very own skin
                                as that   line drawn
                                    in the sand

                dividing the space of   me
                        from all of   everything
                                else   and ...

                        once this division of matter

                became reality –
                        when the me of   myself
                                was   divided out from

                        the All of   Everything else

                        on the other
                                side of
                        my skin ...

                                well,   then

11

                                        the me of   myself
                                                 could be
                                        reduced to

                              the None of   Nothing

                                        and from
                                                 that
                                        came …

… an internal visual representation of myself. I could see my insides as represented
by little bits of color that moved in synchronous harmony, sometimes like the ebb
and flow of the tide and at other times like the swirls of haze rings around the sun.
          Over time I came to collect little bits of colored stones in order to have an out-
side-of-me representation of my insides. There came to be three distinctly separate
piles of little stones: the pastel stones, the solid stones, and the ripple stones.
          Though I didn't become familiar with these little piles of stones in an orderly
fashion, it works to tell their stories in a logical, orderly, and forthright fashion.

                                        and so,
                                             I will …

          My inner Big Bang allowed for a personal reorganization of my inside parts
into what appeared to be three little stone piles. I could perceive this with my inner
eye, that ability that allows me to look inside at my inner parts to see the movements
and sounds connected to them. This enabled me to begin on a journey toward my
place of understanding the

          WHO of me,   the
          HOW of me   and the
          WHAT of me.

          Eventually, this culminated in my understanding of myself as a person with
autism. But that is getting way ahead of this story. Let's return to the beginning of
this personal Big Bang metamorphosis. I want to invite you to come along as I re-
trace the steps of this journey.

          After my personal Big Bang, I started anew, using the clean-slate concept …

          the clean slate of
                    the None   of Nothing

and from   this place of
      clean slate   I pulled out
            from behind   the parts of

            the being of
                  me
            placing them   upon

                  that clean slate
                        in
                  the forefront of   my mind

                        each of these
                              separate pieces of
                        me

            that made up the
                  whole of
            myself

                  becoming represented
                        each piece by
                  a stone

                        pastel stones
                              each stone
                        another of   all of

                              the WHO'S of
                                    me
                              that made up
                                    myself

      … and these pastel stones
                  became
      tucked away

                  in a pocket
                        of
                  her heart

                        always as close
                              as
                        the life of a   heart beat

                              this secret,
                                    yet   then
                              unrevealed content

      of that
            first

<pre>
pile of   stones

             each pastel stone
                     representing
             a WHO   of Her

                 reorganized
                         divided out   from
                 all of   the rest of

                     the matter
                             contained in
                     her universe

    on that
             institutionalized
    teenaged day

         back then
                 when
         that

                 personal
                     Big Bang
                 inside of   her skin

                     explosion of
                             inner
                     universal
                     reorganization,
                             happened
</pre>

     I can remember exactly when this Big Bang happening occurred. At the time, I was a teenager living in a state institution. My roommate had been placed on "elopement precautions" when she was returned to the institution after an attempt to run away. This meant that the overhead fluorescent light in our tiny room had to remain on all night so staff could easily see that my roommate was indeed in her bed and not attempting another escape.

     After 72 hours of being unable to escape the institutional fluorescent lights, I mustered up the where-with-all to begin my own campaign – to escape the assault of the lights at night. I repeatedly asked to be allowed to sleep without the lights on, especially since I had nothing to do with my roommate's elopement attempt. I didn't even know she existed before she was placed in my room after being returned by the police, so in no way could I have been "aiding and abetting," as was usually the assumption applied to the roommate of an eloper.

     It took a few days of campaigning, but finally I was granted my wish to sleep in a dark room. I moved my metal frame cot to the seclusion room at the end of the hall on my ward, looking forward at last to a night without the miserable lights chasing away my sleep. I made up my cot and crawled in, wanting desperately to escape into peace.

But no peace could come to me just then. Instead, my physical experience of the continual day-and-night attack of the fluorescent lights on my body had gotten inside of me! That external "too much" assault had somehow become internalized, resulting in molecules of my very being banging and crashing against each other, picking up speed at an alarming, unstoppable rate.

I lay on the cot rocking my body in attempts to put an outward container around the increasingly frenetic inner energy my body was experiencing. As the ever-escalating intensity reached the physically unbearable point of no return, I allowed my body to succumb, thus becoming transported into the BIG BANG of a physically explosive release.

Ahh ...   what a grandeur
            of release!
                  A physical resolution of
                        unattached   frenetic energy

                  that allowed   waves of
                        peaceful
                  color-oneness

                        to wash   over me
                              in comfort
                        and then ...

                              my body
                                    was
                              ready to

                                    rest   peacefully
                                          through

                        the night,

                  or so I thought.

                  But not so ...

... because an institutional worker would periodically come into the room and awaken me by assaulting my eyes with the piercing shine of a too-bright flashlight. So much for my light-escape campaign and the moving of my cot to the ward seclusion room. That several-day orchestration, though granted, now met with failure, as yet another source of institutional light found a way to assault me.

At the time, I didn't understand that they were merely checking my neurological functions. The experience of my Big Bang was interpreted by the institutional staff as a possible seizure. However, they must not have thought this to be very serious, for the next morning I was sent on an outing with some of the other girls on my ward.

We went to a circus – a literal circus with clowns and elephants, bright spot lights, a trapeze swinger, tigers and monkeys wearing clothes – all infused with alternating attacks of loud, warped circus noises interspersed with hushed awe from the crowd. The experience culminated in a reverberating shot of a cannon, which apparently signaled to the gods the beginning of our being herded back to the bus for a clang-banging, noise-jostling transport back to the state institution.

Upon returning, I walked straight down the hallway of my ward to the aide in the dayroom to ask what had happened to my body the evening before when she had been on duty. I didn't know if this aide had actually witnessed my Big Bang, but assumed she would at least know about it since she had been on duty when it happened. I wanted to know what they called the experience that I had labeled with my current science-class concept of Big Bang Theory.

To my surprise, the aide started shouting and telling me that I knew exactly what I had done – something about my having staged a seizure. She said they knew I had been faking because I had been able to tell the aide her name. Somehow this was taken to mean that I had intentionally staged a seizure.

I couldn't recall even seeing this aide during or after the time of my Big Bang happening, so I wasn't sure what she was talking about. But I realized that it had made her very upset which, in turn, caused her to act quite fussy towards me. It was altogether impossible for me to share any understanding of her experience, seeing that my first recollection after my Big Bang happening had been with a night shift worker shining a flashlight in my eyes.

As a result, my label of Big Bang seemed much more accurate than the world-people label of "staged seizure," especially since, at the time, I didn't even know what a seizure was, much less a staged seizure! Thus, I kept my own very logical and more accurate explanation connotated by my Big Bang label of the event. I also came to the realization that I would not get any more information from the aide AND that it was probably in my best interest not to bring this up with anyone ever again – and until this writing, I haven't.

The good part of all this was that I was allowed to stay in the seclusion room (with my cot still in it) for the rest of the evening so I might think over my misdeed. Ahh … welcome reprieve from the still inwardly manifested outward circus chaos of the day! And what a blessing to also be granted reprieve from the ward with its forever flickering fluorescent dayroom lights and the constant commotion of its 20-plus behaviorally challenged girls.

During this four-hour-long welcome reprieve, I took stock of what the Big Bang had produced inside of me. My insides had become organized in such a way that I could see them and begin to come to an understanding of the parts of me. There were three distinct piles of little stones. The first was made up of several little pieces of pastel-colored bits. When I looked at them, I knew they were all the pieces of the inside unconnected parts of me that had originally been meant to be one whole, but instead looked like little shadow people.

At that time I didn't have any further understanding of this pastel pile of stones. Over time and years of living, the pastel bits opened their arms to me. I discovered they were Me!

The Pastel Stones

Much later in my life, I came to a fuller understanding of the parts of me as represented by the pastel stones. I realized that information learned in one setting didn't automatically transfer to another setting for me, as it seemed to do for the world-people all around me. For example, the "home Judy" might be able to tie shoes and know how to make a sandwich, but the "school Judy" would not be able to access these skills.

Thus, this first pile of stones was comprised of several pastel-colored bits representing the inside unconnected parts of me –

WHO
>   I was   in
>   different places,

>   much of
>   the know-how of
>   the various WHO's

>   unrelated to
>   each other,

>   each WHO
>   of Her
>   represented by

>   a separate
>   pastel bit of
>   colored stone

Over time, as I grew from a child to a teenager, and then into the various stages of womanhood, I was able to look back over the lifetime of these pastel stones. Each of them had its own bit of Me recorded and encapsulated into an entity of its own. These pastel stones held my history, each era distinct and separate from all the others, with none of the content of the stones overlapping.

No wonder I often felt unconnected to my past, as if I was continually starting my life over! I came to understand that this was a function of the way I recorded and stored the happenings of my life – each bit encapsulated in its own entity, never intertwined with any other events. It often felt to me as if I was lost from myself.

When the content of these pastel stones became available to me in my thirties, I was finally able to piece together my past into one whole. During my forties I was able to think of myself as one whole person with a past, a present and a future yet to come. Today I have a good sense of my own personhood, being able to line up the story of each stone chronologically to tell my history and also to imagine forward into the future. I do this by thinking about what the story of the next stone will show. I have to be able to visualize a new pastel stone inside me before I can plan something into the future, like an upcoming vacation, for example.

Here are some of the pastel stones put to words so the reader might better understand how the parts of a person with autism might be portrayed.

Shadow Baby

Hope is haunted   by
      the ghost of

          Shadow Baby's   yester-year existence

      as some children   are haunted
          by ghosts in their   closets

      or dragons   under their beds.

Hope looks back   to see
      a tiny, naked child

          lying in an incubator

      like some hothouse flower
          whose bloom would die

          if touched by human hands.

      Fragile enough to be blown away
          by an exhalation of   breath,

      this child   in a baby-sized box,

          like a coffin
            of glass –

Almost a   nothingness,

      this mere Shadow Baby
          breathed into existence

          on that long ago day.

      Hope lived on

          and   so
          today

          can look back   then.

Shadow Girl

Hope looks back   over time

      to see her   repeatedly plunge
          into   moments of awakening

      all through her   childhood,

    her intelligence gripping the   hand bar
      of a metaphysical teeter-totter

          hanging on   for life   as the ride
      tried to tear   her allegiance   in two

      with its exhilarating flight upward of "I am alive!" and

      it's thrilling plummet through space of "I am alone!"

              versus

      the turmoil of falling back into the world after

      having soared like a winged-thing in that place inside her.

Hope watched   as she often   struggled to   keep

      her tight   hold on that   hand bar.

          Hope made it possible,   even back then,
      for her to   keep   her place in the world

          while she   rode   the teeter-totter
          as Shadow Girl.

Shadow Woman

A rowboat,   washed gently by the waves

    at the edge of the   shore;

a shadow woman   alone inside

    looking out at   the world

       as it was taught   to her –

       a world that didn't always   make sense

           but was quick to   negate

         the reality inside   her.

           That place that never   –   through all of her   life –

              could be snuffed out or   crushed   was private

              and sacred and could   never be touched

              by any   humans outside her.

Hope, looking back   over Shadow Woman's life   to this time

    saw herself awaken   and climb into the boat   beside her.

Taking up the oars, they   set off   together

    On a journey of inside   and outside   discovery.

      Determined not to let   either world negate   the other,

        over time   her Shadow Parts gathered   together,

      making it more comfortable for her   to live in the world –

       Hope now   looking

         both backward and   forward.

The Solid Stones

The second pile of stones was made up of numerous little solid-colored bits. For reasons unknown to me, these solid-colored stones is where the understanding of my inner Big Bang organizational happening first came to rest. Back then, as a teenager in an institution, these were the inside stones that immediately made sense when I looked at them.

So,

here
It is –

the It
that

would one day
become known

as my
autism.

Come along,

read
on,

starting
at

the
place

where
my story

begins
unfolding

with this
second

little
pile

of solid
stones …

The second little pile   of stones
goes back to her beginning

representing inside wiring   of her
very human existence.

She can now see   these stones
            inside her being   having been recreated

                in their now-new   state of
            inner illumination

                at that   yester-year time of
                    Big Bang's   culmination.

Unlike the pastel stones,   these solid stones are not
        parts or pieces   that have   before the time of   her birthing

                split away from   themselves   and are   now waiting
            to be reclaimed   (unbeknownst   even unto   themselves),

                to be righted   melted   fused
        back together,   enabling them

                to become once again   the One of   Her
            instead of their   separate shadow stone   parts,

                unattached to   her being of   self.

But this second pile of stones   you see
        is not anything like the first,

            because instead of showing
                    the inside   unconnected parts of

                    WHO she is,
                they tell a different story.   These stones

                    instead   show
                        just HOW   she is,

                having been   ushered into   inner visibility
                        as the result of   her personally applied

                Big Bang Theory   even though
                        all of them   have always been

                there   residing

                    inside her,

                originally arriving as
                        part of   the package of

                        her birthing.

22

Stone Islands

Stone islands of information
       gently bobbing   suspended
           in the gray-matter space
               of her mind.

Every island born into being
       to support new-growth sprouts of information
          from the world that lived all around her
             on the other side of her skin.

     A system of

          what-to-do-when
              and
          how-to-act-if,

              all info-lands bobbing lazily together,
                  never touching or bumping
             into each other   living together in
                 that same   gray-matter space
of her mind.

Her very own information storage system,
      which wasn't   altogether bad,
          but did have
     its own

              d
              o
              w
              n
              f
              a
              l
              l
              s

          such as the times when   world-information

o

         floated right in her   very midst
                on the other side of   her skin

n

               but then

e

         so were empty islands   f l o a t I n g
               on the inside side of   her skin

d

               tucked in

o

         their own gray-matter suspension

w

n   f l o a t I n g   on by

f

               unavailable for
               world-information implanting

a

l   unable to fulfill
              their mission just then

l

               as in

               "Nowhere to hang your hat."
               (That's funny, so grin!)

Such were the times when world-people
        tried to   force it in,

a

             drill it in,
             drum it in,

n

                all to no avail,
                because

d

precisely at that very moment in time,

a

            there simply just wasn't
            an island available

n

o   f l o a t I n g   on by

t

            for that world-info
               to sink
h   its roots into.

e

Oh, the island was there
          in that gray-matter expanse
r

            (You see,

                there are a bazillion small islands
                empty, awaiting implanting
                suspended in inner eternity.)

          but none had come to lay claim
             to that world-info

                precisely just then
                as was needed.

Some days   new world-info
         quite readily found
         and planted roots down

              on its very own island
              and some days
                    it didn't.

                    But then
              maybe tomorrow or
              next week, month or year
                    (never fear!)

              it wouldn't be a stranger
                    for planting down
                    just as it found
                          on gray-matter horizon

                          an island   home
                    ripe for the taking in

              of orphan world-information
                    embracing its planting
                    nurturing its growth into

              its very own
                    brand spankin' (not really) new
                    set of new rules of

                          what-to-do-when
                                and
                          how-to-act-if
                                and
                          when-to-say-what.

Over time,
      many islands sprouted and grew
           each unto itself –

           each containing its own
             world-living rules.

Once the information had   rooted,
                 sprouted,

            grew   and
            came into its own fullness of being
            on its very own island,

            that island, knowing its very own
            fullness of time

            in its own due time
            (when ready),

            turned in on itself,

              forever preserving
              exact world-rules of

                what-to-do-when
                   and
                how-to-act-if
                   and
                when-to-say-what.

Stone islands
　　forever preserving

　　　　the cast-in-stone
　　　　world-people rules for living

　　never wanting to lose

　　　　the precious bit that was given
　　　　and then so laboriously taken,

　　　　　a precious commodity
　　　　　that when　　accessed appropriately

　　　　　　allows her a part　　in the world-community

　　　　　where world-people lived
　　　　　just over the line

　　　　　on the outside side of her skin.

A storage system

　　of world-info solidified,
　　each bit in its own

　　　　very own island
　　　　of stone,

for all eternity
bobbing gently

in the gray-matter expanse
of her mind,

never to go away,
never to change,

always faithful –

rules to live by
for her whole life long,

rules of

what-to-do-when
and
how-to-act-if
and
when-to-say-what.

… on the inside side of her skin
over that inner gray-matter horizon
lies this conceptual, pictorial world
of inside-her-mind stone islands.

The Ripple Stones

Five kind of smooth, mostly flat stones

with varying rounded edges about them

and ripples

and shades

of butterscotch colors

radiating gently

like pulse beats

across them

is what your eyes see

when you rest them upon

that group of five butterscotch ripple stones

each unique by itself,

yet matching the others,

portraying the senses

that reside within her

on the inside side of that line

(not drawn in sand but)

marked by her skin.

These stones are not as real

as the other two piles of stones

in her inside world

tucked away

in that gray-matter space

of her mind,

but instead these five each unique

matching stones   like portraits

are but a picture,

a marker in time,

if you will.

Stones of importance because

they readily impact

all of

WHO she is

HOW she is

and her perception of

her own life experience and

everything in

and of

and about

the world all around her

the world outside of her being

on the outside   side

of her skin.

So when you see those butterscotch five

ripple stones

not in a pile,

understand they are marking

a place of importance,

each one representing

just one

of the inside-of-her-skin

five senses.

Rippling butterscotch,

each one depicting

one of the following

senses for living:

hearing

seeing

smelling

tasting

and feeling,

each able

to take her

on a journey

of intensity

way too intently.

Hearing Intently*

Always too sensitive,
usually annoying,
overly fine tuned
is her hearing,
making
ordinary human events of the day
like watching TV
too domineering.

The difference
in loudness
from show
to commercial
is so distracting
most days
TV's not
worth it!

In bed
her ears
on the pillows
must be just right
so her heart beat's
loud whooshing
won't keep her awake
all night.

Sometimes
this way
of hearing
comes in quite handy,
like when
strange-sounding car noises
send her preventively
to the mechanic!

One night
on the kitchen counter
she heard
a pill drop.
She
got out of bed
and an overdose
stopped!

It's sometimes
handy
and sometimes
a struggle
when hearing
all
small sounds
is a daily normal.

*From Endow, J. (2006). *Making Lemonade: Hints for Autism's Helpers* (pp. 21-22). Cambridge, WI: Cambridge Book Review Press. Reprinted with permission.

What Stinks and What Doesn't*

Sometimes people think the air smells bad.
They notice it, maybe make a comment,
but then soon forget it

as their attention focuses
back to whatever their previous business

of the day happened to be
before they noticed the odor.

For her, bad smells are a bit more intrusive.
She notices them more quickly than others
and sometimes can smell

what nobody else
ever seems to notice.

When the stench is bad
in the atmosphere
on the outside of her skin,

it takes her attention
until she can discover

a way to cope with the stink
or else somehow end it.

But she's become smart about stink.
She now stops to think
and to remind herself quite often

that nobody else
will want to know

what stinks to her
and what doesn't!

*From Endow, J. (2006). *Making Lemonade: Hints for Autism's Helpers* (p. 26). Cambridge, WI: Cambridge Book Review Press. Reprinted with permission.

Barometers for Measuring Inside Feelings

As an adult I wrote about how my insides had become reorganized back then, during the time when I was an institutionalized teenager. This Big Bang explosion of my insides and the resulting pictorially exposed internal organization allowed me the opportunity to learn about myself. I shared the story of my stones with another, who promptly inquired, "Are the stones your feelings?"

To answer this question I decided to use paper words – writing on paper the words that matched my inner experience. As of then, I had not yet heard about autism. But, once again, that is getting ahead of the story …

So now, back to the journey …

I once again invite you
                to come   walk along

                with me
                as my world of

                        autism
                        becomes

"discovered" …

"Are the stones your feelings?"
        she asked.

        "No, they are not,"
                was my reply.

        And later
                I wrote …

The second pile of stones

    are her islands of information

        about

    how things (in the world) work

        and

    how people (in the world) expect her to respond

            in acts   and

            in words   and

            in deeds,

                indeed.

These stones are hard   very hard

    just like   concrete,   representing concrete information

      that doesn't change

      but stays the same

          forever.

Feelings are something else.

    There are no stones to show them.

      In her inside world   feelings are

  measured by   an intensity barometer   similar to

      what's used to   measure

  atmospheric pressure   of the weather.

Barometer development over time,

this is how it went:

The first barometer was   white and black.

white = good

black = bad   (and later mad,

which then made white   be glad

and   later still …

It's always better   to keep your cool …

never good   to blow your stack).

The first choices   were simple

and only two   *either* it was one   *or*

the other

the weather barometer registering

white   or black,

which meant   her mood   was cold   or stormy

(which, in turn, caused world-people   to believe that

she was rather oblivious   of all

that happened   around her,

not caring

to connect   with others   or

to be

a part of   the world.

This wasn't true   even though

it was

the way   things truly were

because

as of yet there   wasn't   barometer development

enough   to help connect

her human soul   to others.)

Over time   barometer development did   happen

because   there was   too much   to lump

into   only two   choices   of

this one   or   the other.

That is when

Barometer Two came   into being,

and with it came   its shades   of gray.

Her choices were   e x p a n d i n g

from this one   or the other

to include   gray spaces

in the middle.

The concept of intensity   was able   to be shown,

but different kinds of   feelings

at this very early stage

were entirely yet   unknown.

To recap,   so far in barometer development we have:

Barometer One   with its white or black choices   and

Barometer Two   with its shades of gray.

The logical next barometer to be

would likely be named

Barometer Three   but it isn't   because

it's not any different from

Barometer Two   with   graduated shades

of intensity.   The differences lie

in the color choices,

causing the next   barometer to be

not Barometer Three   but

Barometer Two Refracted.

Blackness is made from the blending of

all of our   color choices,   which means that

when we perceive   white   or black

what we are really seeing   is

white   or all the colors   packed

together

into one space,

making black.

Thus, Barometer Two Refracted is   just that …

      the space of black

        refracted back

      into the separate colors it   came from.

She bent her eyes   until

     she saw   the space of black

     refracted

   and then   could match   the feeling words

     (that world-people were hell bent on teaching)

   to the reality of   her experience.

And this is how she did it:

     world-people's   feeling words   were each

      made into a label,

       which   she then put

    into   her pocket.   And

       over time,

     as the colors of life   became present

      on the horizon

      deep inside her,

     she sifted through   her pocket labels

      and   picking one

    that matched

      she attached it   until

her inside colors   were labeled

with world-people's

names   for feelings.

And each of these   colors of black refracted

had their own shades in   their middle

not shades of gray   but shades

of their very own color

in hues graduated.

She came to know   after a very   l o n g   time   that

her experiences with the shades

of each color's   refraction

could be translated   into world-people's language

like this:

colors = feelings

shades of color = varying intensities of each feeling

So, there you have it –

Barometer Two Refracted.

With barometer development   over time

she came to know what to call   her colors

by using   world-people language   for feelings.

Today

the barometers show   different colors   and

their varying hues and shades

their substance

now easily able

to be translated

into words of feelings   with varying intensities

(most of the time   discernible

to her

but not always

as of yet.

Maybe this   will get even better,

and   maybe not.

Just now   it might be

as good as it gets,

but nevertheless,

this is what she's got

for today.)

Internal Communication Connections

I remember with fondness my institutional social worker and some of my favorite aides who began group therapy sessions with a handful of girls on my ward. The topic was often the same – FEELINGS.

I understood feelings intellectually, knowing their labels and their definitions. I also began to realize that the way I perceived the world – through the movements and sounds of colors …

though real   as real

          could be

                    to me

          was not

                    a reality   shared

                              by others

                    and thus …

I came to understand that if I wanted one day to be discharged from this institution, it behooved me NOT to share my color realities with others. So, I didn't.

Instead, I focused on learning all I could about feelings so that I might figure out how to match this information to my perceived experiences with my beloved colors. And yes, colors were my "beloved," because through the movements and sounds of colors I was able to make my way in the world outside of my skin. Because of my perceptions of the ways of the colors all around me and the colors generated from the interactions between people, I began to pay more attention – and thus came to a better and better understanding of the world-people world around me. Thus, as a teen I was able to begin to very literally sort out and apply the feeling labels I carried around in my pocket to the colors of my then-current life experiences.

Today I write this because I want world-people to understand that actual barometer development happened in a very literal and concrete way for me. I also would like it if people could start to imagine a world perceived by the movement and sounds of colors rather than a world whose meaning is primarily obtained by the sound of words being articulated.

And while you are imagining, please entertain the notion that a person who has an internally wired neurology to enable this, though a bit different from most, may not be any less intelligent, or indeed any less of a human being, than the typically wired folks, who are clearly in "The Majority" in the world-people world that we all inhabit.

It may not be any better or any worse …

It is just different.

(But, for real, does "different" and "minority" need to be equated with "less than"?)

And still, at this point in the story, I had not yet become acquainted with autism. Indeed, my "communicative" brand of autism had not yet become widely known in the world outside my skin.

But just because others didn't yet know about IT

and therefore I could not be told about IT

or have any way to become acquainted with IT,

I nevertheless kept right on discovering this IT

that would one day come to be called my AUTISM.

So,   once again,

come   along
        with me
            on my   journey
                of discovery …

                of my own   private
                    world   that resides

            in that   inside space
                    of the place   on
                        the side of
                    my skin   that's located on
                    the inside
                            side of   me.

                This   private world
                        of mine
                    that would
                        one day

                come to   be called

                    my autism …

44

Bridge Pieces
(Information Storage)

The stone island stones

in that   inside-my-mind space   have

little bridge pieces

jutting off them

in varying places

from their surface

of stone.

Pieces of bridges,

but never   a whole bridge,

connecting any   two surfaces

of two different islands   each one containing

its very own specific information

set in stone for one

and only for one

specific eventuality

learned from life previously

recorded historically

immovable, unchangeable

set as set can be

in stone island

cemented reality

encapsulated,

preserved

for all time

forever,

eternally,

with no bridges connecting –

no way of sharing

one island's info

with any other.

That's why there are   g   a   p   s

in that gray-matter space of her mind's place where

she knows bridges should be

but are not

there to connect this info

with that   and, therefore,

no way

to extrapolate

info from one

specific, circumstantial

island of stone

and apply it

to something a little bit

slightly different

that might be occurring

just now

in her life.

Sometimes she becomes quite frustrated

when she finds herself in a new situation

and isn't able to gather together, sift, and apply

bits of info from several stone islands

already in existence,

bobbing around,

      each one minding

its own business –

never connecting

      each their own info

one with another

because they can't

      with only bridge pieces –

no whole bridges anywhere

to be found

      between islands

      to span

all the   g a p s.

If only world-people could see into

   •   that gray-matter space of her mind

a suspension of matter

that matters because

      it supports

her many islands of stone

each one with their purpose

      of holding

pertinent, specific

world-information of

what-to-do-when

and

how-to-act-if

and

when-to-say-what

solid information cast in stone

solidified in place

in that gray-matter space

of her mind.

Then world-people might see the little bridge pieces

stuck onto the sides of all these stone islands.

Bridge pieces just hanging there serving no purpose

(other than to <u>underline</u> the fact that
a bridge was meant to be there, but isn't)

little bridge pieces going nowhere

with gray-matter g a p s

where the bridges should be.

Perhaps then the world-people might come to understand

that even though

she may know

all the info that's needed

to answer their question

or to produce a reciprocal response

to keep up with her part of their conversation,

sometimes it takes a lot of her time

to jump in a boat and float around

    in that gray-matter space of her mind

    floating in the   g a p s   trying to find

        all the right islands of stone

        that might hold any relevant data

            pertinent to the subject at hand.

        Sometimes it's a cumbersome task

            to access information in this manner

            and at other times it is downright impossible.

It's at these times when she knows that she knows

        all of the relevant data

    and desperately tries to locate it   and can't

        she knows that she knows,

        but can't tell you right now   at this very minute

            exactly what it is

            (and she may not even know it an hour from now)

        because what she needs can't be fit together

        to make any logical sense.

            Please try to remember

            she's dealing with   g a p s

            because there simply are no bridges.

And at these particular times she tends

to look very directly at the person who is talking to her

(as if she might find what she's looking for by staring intensely into that person's eyes

Sometimes she gets a goofy little half-grin

(or so she's been told, but as for herself never noticed this).

During this time   she's marking time

waiting for the info she needs   to come in

hoping to be able to fill in the   g a p s   in time

with the info she knows that she knows,

but try as hard as she might,

right now she can't find.

Invariably an exasperated, superior world-person will declare with finality,

"YOU KNOW EXACTLY WHAT YOU'RE DOING!"

and disgustedly walk away.

But if he doesn't leave too fast,

he might hear her agree,

because after all she already knows that she knows,

but just doesn't know what it is

(or if she is told   the info she is lacking,

she can   and may   even repeat it back,

but to her,

even the right info,

supplied as it may be

by frustrated

world-people,

has no

present meaning

to her

and, therefore,

cannot   be applied

right now

to this   particular

situation in

today's reality).

She tries very hard   to be acceptable

she may even be able   to say the right words,

repeating what someone   outside her supplied.

But her understanding is   blank just then.

She really can't help it:

she has

g   a   p   s

not bridges.

The Gaps
(Information Processing)

When the   g a p s   are what she's getting

    after searching through her stone islands of information,

        she experiences a huge frustration

    but tries hard not to let anyone know it

        by trying to ensure her behavior won't show it

    so nobody will know that she's coming up empty,

        not able to supply whatever it is they are after,

    whatever it is they want her to know

        (and she probably does, but can't tell what it is just then).

Most of the time she wants to join in

    to take her place   (or any place!)   in the world,

        but she's "drawing a blank," as that expression goes,

    because the   g a p s   are so empty.

    She doesn't want to be empty.

    She'd rather be friendly.

She tries to join in.

She may laugh or smile,

       but in a short while

       all the world-people are mad again.

And that is how it is most of the time

   when she tries to take part

       and act like they want her to act.

         She can for a while,

         but then "draws a blank"

         when the   g a p s   come up

         where there should be bridges.

Canoe Transportation
(Information Retrieval)

Hard stone islands of   information solidified

       with little bridge pieces jutting   off their sides

           suspended inside

           the gray-matter space

             of her mind

       Islands of information each   unto themselves

          not able to share their   information

          one island with   another   because

             the little bridge pieces

             jutting off their sides

             never did grow   to form any bridges

               as they were originally   meant to.

When she needed info

      from more than   one island,

         it became very difficult   to gather

        with no bridges to span the g a p s

           in that gray-matter space

           between her bazillion

             inside-her-mind stone islands.

Slowly, over time she constructed   a boat

     so that she might float   about

          in that gray-matter space of her mind

          to gather up info,

             stone island by island.

       The boat took ever so long to construct   because

          there were no   raw materials,

          nothing to use to build a boat with

             in that   inside-her-mind space

             filled up with

               stone islands.

She started to watch outside of   her skin

     to see what she could find

          to build a stone island boat with.

       It was tricky because   she couldn't use

          any boards or nails   that were

          outside of her skin in the world   to drag

             into that gray-matter space

             of her inside-her-mind

               world of stone islands.

And yet, she needed materials

    she could use to build a boat

    that she could then climb inside of

       and float in from island   to island

       gathering bits and pieces   of world-info needed

        when she needed to assimilate

        all of the relevant data

          pertinent to some current, given,

          relative now, in-front-of-her-face

            everyday commonplace

            world-conversation situation.

Over time she discovered   that   **if**

    she could live in

       an outside-her-skin

       world of specific order,

        not left to chance,

        it gave her a chance

          to be able to travel

          between her

            stone islands.

What worked best was to stick to a schedule

    the same schedule   every day

so she always would know   ahead of time

just exactly what to expect.

          And the more she could keep things the same

          in the world outside of her skin,

                    the better the chance that her boat would float

                    rather than sinking down in

                              the gray-matter space

                              of the inside-her-mind place

                                        of that stone island world inside her.

Her boat began to look like a canoe   with

          two sides and a seat in the middle.

          One side of her canoe was her daily schedule

          that she tried to keep the same   each day

                    as much as she was humanly able.

          The other side of her canoe   was constructed

          as a result of

                    her scavenger hunting in places outside of   her skin

                    where world-people walk and talk

                              and seem comfortable living in.

She made a habit of listening in

    on this world-people space

        that was all over the place   just over the line

        on the other side   the outside side

          of her skin.

          She became a scavenger on the lookout   for

            bits and clues that might show her

            just what to expect ahead of time

              before it would actually happen

              in that world-people world

                right outside her.

The more bits and clues that she could pick up   and use,

    the stronger that side of her boat became   until

        it matched in strength

        the other side   that was built

          with her daily schedule.

Then she found that for her to sit down

    in this boat of two sides she had built

        she needed a seat upon which to sit

        because if she stood up

          the boat would tip

dumping her out   into the   g a p s

of gray-matter space

making her flail about desperately

going nowhere except

sinking down

drowning inside of herself.

One day she discovered   quite by accident

that in her boat she sat

on a seat that   had constructed itself

out of her matching habits.

It very much surprised her

when she looked at the boat seat   and saw

her morning activities

spread between boat sides,

building the boat seat in the middle

right before her

very own eyes!

She had:

matched the socks in her sock drawer

and folded all her pants the same.

Her clean sheets and pillowcase were a set,

and the colors of her clothes matched each other.

In the cafeteria she noticed all the plates were the same,

and the silverware matched together.

All the cups were green. All the trays were brown

and all the kids sat down

at exactly the same kind of

little square tables.

After studying the boat seat,

she was able to discover just how it had been made.

When everything matched and looked the same   in the

outside-her-skin   world-people world,

she could sit back and relax

in a comfortable way

on the inside side of her skin.

Sitting like this in her boat, she could float

in gray-matter space between islands,

finding islands containing

the info she needed

right in each moment of time …

her previously stored, cast in stone,

forever preserved, encapsulated

world-people information of

what-to-do-when

and

how-to-act-if

and

when to say what.

Because of this two-sided boat

with its seat in the middle,

stone island info

was now retrievable.

Once I learned the process of retrieving the information I had previously stored inside me, my life began to take on new meaning. I began to feel less isolated, and sometimes even had glimpses of wondering if I was maybe human and maybe even meant somehow to be a part of something bigger than myself …

Glimpses …
only glimpses …
of possibly wanting to

one day connect

with a world outside of
my skin   a world that

was foreign
and still
my
autism

as of yet
unknown

while my
inner reality

summed up
was

expressed
like this …

Stone islands

each   unto themselves

not naturally   connecting

to one another

not able   to share

their information

even though,

after so

many years,

much info

could now

(if the system had been set up differently)

be   overlapping.

If only …

the islands

could   touch

each other;

but   not so

    'cause   they can't …

It's sometimes   a rather cumbersome system

    to store   world-info

    independently,

    as each

    little bit

    comes in

    never   connecting

    later info   to

    anything former,

    but encapsulating instead

    each   world-info   rendering

    into   its own

separate island

    eventually turning

    itself   to stone

    suspended into

    the gray-matter space

    of her mind

    on the inside side

    of her skin

    but then …

She didn't have a vote

on which system   got wired

as she was constructed   into person-hood

in that time before birth.

Indeed, she didn't know how uncommon

her inside wiring   for storing

world-information   was

to most of the people on earth.

During nine months of gestation

she was wired this way   (like an electronic map of sorts),

which later made her   appear to be

an alien dropped into the earth.

Not fitting in –

was that such a sin (?)

since God wired her to be   an inside person

sojourning the earth –

clearly an odd

incompatibility

with omnipresent

world commonality,

but construct this

she didn't.

She couldn't change   the world,

    and she couldn't change   her wiring,

    so this is what   she did:

      an imaginary line   she drew –

        a demarcation

        between   the two.

Over time

    her very own skin

    became   this line.

      World-people   and all

        that belonged   to them

        were on   the other side,

          outside   side of her skin.

While all   that made sense

    to her   very being …

      information islands

      with bridge pieces   forming

        and barometers   for measuring

        her inside feelings.

      These ideas   expressing

        her reality

        became   more than people;

they were   her family,

her kin,   because

    to these   ideas

    (not people)

she attached …

    all located

    within,

    on the inside side

    of her skin.

    Amen!

CHAPTER TWO

NOTICING

MY

DIFFERENCES

As a teen confined to a state mental institution I was extremely quiet. In fact, I went for a long time without talking at all. It wasn't that I couldn't talk; I simply didn't. I was diagnosed with depression by the psychiatrist.

My family talked about my "nervous breakdown," which led me to believe that the nerves inside my body had quite literally broken down – similar to the way a car breaks down. When a car begins breaking down, it still runs but just doesn't perform correctly. When a car has a complete breakdown, it stops running altogether and doesn't perform at all. Therefore, using this broken down car analogy, my logical assumption was that my nerves must have been starting to break down when I had been hospitalized on the psych ward near my hometown. Now that I was at the faraway state institution, it made sense that this meant that the nerves in my body had somehow completely broken down; thus the term "nervous breakdown." I was very thankful that there was no physical pain involved when my nerves broke down. Indeed, I had never felt a thing and wouldn't even be able to tell you which day, never mind the precise moment, when my "nervous breakdown" occurred.

Furthermore, I assumed that since my nerves had broken down, it would be expected, and therefore perfectly fine, that I stopped talking. Besides being a great relief not to have to perform all the internal mechanical tasks that go along with using speaking words, it led to quite a functional strategy for me! Rather than using up much of my daily energies on all that speaking entailed, I could instead use my energies to look inside myself in search of the broken nerves. It seemed logical that the place of the break would need to be discovered and reported before the hospital workers could set about fixing this break.

Most of the time my inner being looked like a jumbled muddle, but once I spent a few months without talking, the muddle started untangling itself. The more the muddle untangled, the better I was able to see my internal wiring. I thought I was looking at my broken nerves and that it was important to record and report my findings to my doctor. I imagined that he would use my information to somehow help mend my broken nerves. So I did my part – now recorded as the first chapter of this book – much of the chapter you just finished reading. Unfortunately, the doctor never did his part, at least the part that I had imagined he would do.

It took me a long time to figure out that nobody at the institution was interested in my personal discoveries about how my nerves were wired inside my body. Initially, my belief had been that if the doctor read what I wrote, he would have the information necessary to fix up my broken nerves. I further believed that as soon as he became privy to the information, he would get right to fixing me up.

Because I was so sure of this, and because he wasn't at all interested in reading what I wrote, I began speaking again just so I could tell him of my discoveries. I knew spoken words were his preferred mode of receiving information and thought I had important information and should accommodate him. For several months, I tried my best to get him to understand, even though I was only granted fifteen minutes of his time once or twice each month.

Looking back, I am certain that this is the point when it was decided that I was delusional and having hallucinations. I had been insisting that I could see the nerves inside my body. I repeatedly told every staff member I could get to listen how my internal wiring, along with its hookups, looked inside of me. None of the staff on my ward seemed to want to hear about my phenomenal discovery, even though I tried to tell each and every one of them many, many times!

When I finally got to tell the doctor about it, he hardly listened. Initially, I thought he didn't want to know about my discovery. Then, when his only comment was that he wanted me to take a new pill, I figured that he didn't need to know from me about my discovery because the ward staff had already reported my findings to him. That made sense, especially since I knew that my discovery of how my nerves were wired inside my body was breakthrough information, undoubtedly helpful to the doctor in remedying my "nervous breakdown."

I was excited about getting a pill that would mend the breaks in my nerves and expressed this to the med nurse. She informed me that the pill was to stop my hallucinations.

The pills turned out to be awful. At first I lost the ability to tell where my body was in relationship to everything else in the room. Then, I began feeling as if I was physically melting into my surroundings, becoming part of the air around me rather than the separate physical entity of a human being. Finally, after a few days, I lost track of my very being. I didn't catch up with myself until several months later when they stopped having me take the pills. Once my use of the pills had been tapered and stopped, I realized that three whole months of my life had escaped me.

This harrowing experience made me understand that to survive the institution, I would need to change my strategy. I needed to NOT write or talk about the broken nerves inside my body. Even though I was certain this information was vitally important, it seemed even more important by then to keep it a secret. So I did. I never again tried to write or talk about the way the wiring of the nerves in my body looked to me. I had learned my lesson; this talk would be equated with hallucinations, and consequently I would be medicated. Never again did I go back to those thoughts until the writing of this book.

Today I can appreciate that back then I was describing the neurology of my own autism, but back then there was no autism label available for the doctor to apply to somebody like me, who was able to talk. It was a piece of science not yet discovered. I believe my doctors did the best they could within the framework of the diagnostic choices available to them in the mid 1960s.

So even though I figured out NOT to talk about my internal wiring, so as to avoid heavy-duty psych meds, I remained of the opinion that this was important information. I started realizing that if I were to ever get out of the institution, I would need to "act normal," whatever that meant.

In practical terms, I thought that if I could pinpoint the ways in which I was different from the other teenage girls on my ward, I could learn to hide my differences. I was convinced this new strategy would be my discharge ticket.

It came to pass that my assumption was correct. I discovered several ways in which I was different from other teenage girls on my ward and then learned how to hide those differences. Lucky for me, I eventually got discharged!

In the meantime, I went on a fact-finding mission to discover how I was "different." I had become aware that the doctor and the staff, just as they had no intentions of figuring out where my nerves were broken so they could fix them, also had no intentions of figuring out my differences so they might fix them. Instead, their agenda seemed to be wrapped up in using behavior modification with rewards and punishments to cause the patients, including me, to come to choose to "act normal."

It became apparent to me that in order to succeed in this behavior mod setup, I would first have to figure out how I was different from my peers. Once I had that information, it would be easy to find out how to hide my differences so as to appear "normal."

So, as the second year of my institutional stay began, I put my efforts into this new project, keeping it secretive lest they decide to try another psych med on me. In the process, I came to rely on my big blanket. It enabled me to write about my discoveries of the ways in which I was different from others. I found that when I rolled myself up tightly in my blanket, the pressure it created against my body helped keep me relaxed enough to focus on my differences.

From as far back as I can remember, being able to squish my body always produced a calming effect. Back then I didn't understand why, and neither did anyone else. They only tried to get me to stop because my behavior around squishing myself wasn't "normal." Today, in the field of autism, the benefits of deep pressure are understood, and accommodations are often put into place to enable people to get their deep-pressure needs met in a safe manner.

Coming to learn about my own autism was still a long way off. Even so, I used the strategy of rolling myself tightly into a blanket to enable me to feel physically comfortable enough to focus on my differences. Many years later I discovered that a canvass and Velcro™ device used for restraint purposes allowed me to roll myself up more tightly than what a blanket allowed. (This is not something that is recommended to be done at home due to safety issues, so please do not try this without medical supervision.) And thus, I wrote the poems in this chapter of the book you are now reading.

Come journey   with me.
        Read the words that I wrote

                about the facts
                of my differences

                words

                        matching   my realities
                        discovered and written

        from

                inside a burrito …

Inside a Burrito

Inside a burrito

wrapped tightly up

her body can feel

pressure all around it

as she   breathes air

into her body

the sensation   of pressure

is enhanced   in a way

that causes   her skin to   know

experientially   just where

she is inside   of her skin,   which is now

inside the   burrito wrapper

all wrapped   right up

tightly.

this   pressure sensation

is like a   craving   she's yearned after

her whole life   long   and

just now has discovered   and is   rejoicing

to have found   that this craving

can ultimately be   satisfied

when she is

wrapped up   tight as tight   can be,

becoming the   inside part of

a human burrito

inside of the   canvass and Velcro™   restraint

   initially taking   the very deepest   breaths

    specifically trying   to   intensify

      the pressure   being created

    against the outside of   her skin

     when she is   wrapped up

       tightly inside   a burrito

after a while   when   her pressure needs

  become more satisfied

    she doesn't have to breathe   so deeply

     as her craving   recedes   inside her,

  she breathes with   a slower

   more normal rhythm,

    allowing each intake   of air

 to push   her body

   up snug   against

    the outside   burrito wrapper

in time she   relaxes   and if

  she so chooses

   when she's   snuggly relaxed

    all comfortably squished together

 she can   look at

   old pictures inside her

    that shows

all those times   when others

            have noticed   her differences   in such a way

                        that brought   pain and frustration   to her

but now   when she's safely relaxed   inside a burrito

            she can walk   right into

                        old photos   being able to

see through   today's eyes   of understanding

            and able to   readily translate

                        yesterday's pictures

into words   for today   that

            she sincerely hopes

                        will be meaningful   to others.

So, if you   are a person

            who may want   to know about

                        some aspects of living with autism,

                        for whatever   might be   your reason,

then the words   of this chapter

            are a gift   to you   from her

                        very literally   written

while wrapped tightly up

            snuggled down deep

                        inside a burrito

The Facts of the Matter

all her life alone
    only with   herself
        no   outside person   understanding

    the autistic   longings and
        unspoken wishes   residing inside her

    referred to as "oddities"

        by those people
            outside of her skin
        who have been given
            the power   to label
                her differences

all her life alone
    not ever able to tell   someone else
        because if she did   they would

    feel sorry for her
        because from their   frame of reference

    being alone   one's whole life

        not often
            feeling understood
        would be
            an awful
                tragedy

but for her,   "all her life alone"
    doesn't hold
        that kind of   significance

    it's more   like a fact
        about   how she is,

    which happens to be

most often
     alone
in a world
     full of people
          all   around her

"all her life alone"
    is a fact   about her
        that she doesn't   interpret

  as   good or bad
     but tends to think of   in terms of

    being how   she is,

      meaning quite simply
        this state of affairs

    has no emotional component

       but is   quite simply   no more than

        the very plain fact   of   the matter

Much of the Time—
From Back Then to Just Now

much of the time

    not having a friend

      not being a friend

        not wanting a friend

          not needing a friend

          was her growing-up thoughts
          but no longer today's experience

still not knowing why this is,

    only knowing that it was

      that during her growing up years
      friends were just not important

        and over time   she became

        comfortable with

          this seemingly odd   indifference

not needing to   talk

    yet wanting to   be heard

      easily   getting tangled up

        in words   with more

          than one   meaning

yet using words to
write down ideas effectively

not always understanding

    words people are speaking

        yet able to match

           their insides   quite readily

              every deficit balanced
              with a blessing

sometimes looking odd

    or presenting as challenging

        perceived as difficult when   she's only trying

          to keep the world   sorted out

            when it's   jumbled up
            outside her

People Are for a Purpose

Writing from Back Then:

people are for a purpose
      rather than   to form   friendships with

talking to them is   for a reason
      rather than   to get to   know them

        so when   there is no reason   for conversation
          she tends to   have no words

      but when there is   a purpose   for what she   says
        her words can   go on   forever

         especially if   she never
      knows   when her   intent

        has been   accomplished

Writing from Just Now:

it's often hard for her   to get started   with words
      making it difficult   to leave a   spontaneous message

after   the machine goes beep
      sometimes causing   others to become   quite frustrated

      (like that "friend"   with her caller ID)

        but when she has   a reason to   speak
   she says   her words   over and over

       as many times as   it takes
         until she can know   that her words

       found a home   inside of
         the other   person's body

       connecting to   their inside place
         of understanding

Writing for All Time:

others tend to   experience this
      as her persistence or   her stubbornness

depending upon   their own
     patience and   tolerance

       in accommodating her   difference

         sometimes she   gives up
     when she   can't find

        the other person's insides   connecting
        with   the words she's saying

her speaking words   abruptly stop
     maybe even in   mid sentence

       when she can't   find
   a way   to match

      with   the other person's
       inside space

       her words   just quit
        when she   can't find

         a place to put   them into

       a word container
        found

          inside of   another

The Purpose of People

the purpose of people
    in her life

        are many
           and varied

        such as

        people to go to school with
        people who teach music lessons

        people who cut hair
        people to play with

        people to give presents to
        people to accept treats from

        people to use good manners with
        people to make things for

        people to go to the library with
        etc., etc., etc.

all the people who   she lives out   her life with
    fit into   specific categories

        each with a given   purpose

    sometimes individual people   are
        in more than   one category

        but this doesn't   happen   very often

it becomes disconcerting   to her
    when people try   to expand or change   their categories

        like the time in her adult life when   a person   she worked with

    asked if   he could   take her out to dinner
        her answer was   very simple:

        "NO"

this person became   offended
        even though   she never intended

                to offend him

    in fact   she thought he was   rather nice
            and had even come   to like him

                but he was someone   she worked with

when he asked her   to dinner   it meant
        e x p a n d I n g   the categories

            this person   could   fit into

    and she could have   done that
            but not in   an instant   when   the expectation

                was an   immediate answer

so, her default mode   kicked instantly   in
        which is   what happens whenever   she's put   on the spot

            in default   her answer is always   "NO"

    because it   immediately stops   perceived chaos
            and effectively keeps   the world   all around her

                in its proper balance

About "No"

her answer to questions
    or to new situations

        when she's   not given

    the time she needs   to travel around
        and gather   all
            the right   information

    inside her

        pertaining to   the topic
            at hand

        is always very   predictable

her immediate answer
    to any question   expecting one

        is either   "NO" or
                "I DON'T KNOW"

    and there isn't   any other
        answer she   will give

    to any question   or situation   that's
        new   to her

        not previously   thought out   and
        responded to   enough times   to

        have become   a part   of some
            predictable pattern   inside her

she knows this   often causes   her
    to appear   stupid   when

    she isn't

professionals often   call
    her manner of   relating

        noncompliant   or
oppositional-defiant

        depending upon

            whether

      her role
          in their case

                is that   of

          "mother-of-child"
              or
              "client"

How Making Things Better Worked Back Then

she has noticed   most people   outside her
      turn to   other people   for comfort

      when either   the outside or the inside of them   becomes upset

      this seems   peculiar to her   and maybe   it wouldn't
      if it wasn't   their   first line of defense   against

      an inside or outside upset

this is how   things work   for her
      when she needs   to find comfort

      or needs   to soothe herself

      when the inside   or outside of her   becomes upset
      and she   must restore   a balance

#1   her FIRST LINE OF DEFENSE against

      those things outside her   that "rile her up"

      or the inside   upsets
      that are   difficult to handle

      is this:

#1a   if the upset's INSIDE her   she finds
      something soothing to look at
      with either a repetitive pattern
      or colors that match

      when she looks at these things
      they tend to restore
      the upset inside balance

#1b   if the upset's OUTSIDE her such as
        too many things out of place,

        noises too loud or a lot of commotion
        the solution is simply to fix it –

        to make it look or sound better
        will take care of the problem

#2   her SECOND LINE OF DEFENSE

    to restore her balance
        goes like this:

#2a   if the upset's INSIDE her   she must
        stay put together   quite literally meaning

        that when her insides   start feeling   like
        they are coming unglued   from each other

        she must   somehow ensure
        that they stay   stuck together

        so this is what she does:
            -move away from people
            -go into another room
            -go some place to be alone
            -stop and just sit still
                with no outside distraction

            all of these strategies   work to make
            her jittery insides   settle back down

            and stick back together
            the way they belong

        this usually takes 3-5 minutes
        and if   she's around other people

        she excuses herself
        to go use the bathroom

#2b   if the upset's OUTSIDE her
        and trying to fix it didn't work

        she must make a plan
        to move somewhere else

        if she's already alone
        it's quite simple to move   but

        if she's in the   company of others
        she must   quickly discover   a way

        to socially   appropriately   move
        not only herself   but all of   the others

        sometimes this can work   and sometimes it can't
        in which case she   endures it

        as long as   she possibly   can
        while   in the meantime   getting ready

        a reason   to use   if she reaches
        her tolerance and   needs to be   excused

#3   her THIRD LINE OF DEFENSE

    she isn't as well acquainted with   (Back Then during this writing) since
        she rarely tried to use it   and therefore

        didn't always know   just how
    to   deal with it   except   to somehow

        very literally   physically squish
    her insides   back together

        because this   she truly did know
    would work   when all else failed to

        restore   to her   both
    her inside and outside   balance

and these are the times
when she might look   to other people   for help
these times when she's become beside herself

      (because   her insides feel   as if
      they have   come out of her
      and are now   next to her
      right along side of   beside herself)

it's only now   that other people   might possibly be
a comfort to her   but only if they can understand   and

somehow provide   a way to get
her insides squished   back together again

so one of the ways   she is different   from
    most of the   people around her

      is WHEN   (at what point   in distress)
   she might   turn to others   for comfort

      to possibly help   when there is   an upset
  either outside   or inside   her

Writing Scripts Ahead of Time*

when new situations arise in her life
    often   she is silent
        and without reaction
    simply because   there is   no reaction   inside her

a long time ago   she figured out
    that it's really not   a good idea
        to be like   a magician   pulling a rabbit   out of a hat

    and just   pull out   any old   behavior
      already inside her   and apply it
        to something new   that's happening today

      because   whenever she used that magician strategy
      it never worked   very well –

        she always got   some strange animal
      never the   expected rabbit –

        which then   caused people
          to act strangely   towards her,
      to call her   crazy   or
        to just   not like her

from watching   all the world-people   all around her
    she discovered

      that   all sorts of behaviors
    even the   new ones   they had never yet tried

      somehow
      had already
      been placed
        inside them

after watching   for a long time
    she finally   decided
      that   all of   the world-people
    must have been   made this way

from   the very beginning

    even before
  they were born

she didn't know why she was made differently

 but even if she   did know
  it   wouldn't really much matter

 as right then
   she just needed to figure out a way
    to get new behaviors
  put inside her

    before the time came
     to search through all of her
   "how-to-react-behavior-data"

    in tomorrow's future
     when she would need
    to find it

in order for her to act in a new way
  the behavior desired

   must have somehow
been previously placed
  inside her

   the idea being quite simple:

 in order to retrieve the data
   it must first be entered

next she had to figure out
  how to enter the data

  without ever knowing
 what the data might be

  in order to discover

what the   data that were missing
inside her   might be

she   watched all the   world-people
outside her   to see

how they behaved
when they   were together –

what   they said
and how   they acted
towards   each other

then   whenever   she liked   what she saw
she made   a story

always in the same order

like this:
1.   situation …
2.   what to say …
3.   how to act …

and when   the story   was finished
she put her name   in it

and   that is how   she entered
unknown data inside her

ahead of the time   when she   might someday need it …

before that   tomorrow-time came   to search   through all of
her   "how-to-react-behavior-data"

that had already   been previously
placed and stored   inside her –

by writing   the scripts   ahead of   the time
she would   act them out

just in case   she would
one day   need them

*From Endow, J. (2006). *Making Lemonade: Hints for Autism's Helpers* (pp. 52-54). Cambridge, WI: Cambridge Book Review Press. Reprinted with permission.

Making New Pictures

her thoughts and ideas
    are not made   with words

        but instead   she has pictures
          inside her head

        that pop up   on a screen
          every time   she thinks

            of something   she knows about
            or has   previously seen

for those things   she is pondering
    and hasn't   yet seen

        there isn't   a picture
          that can   pop up   on her screen

       because   at that time
         there hasn't   yet been

          a picture constructed
            and stored   in her head

       for her   to retrieve
         that shows the   new idea

          that she is   right now
           wondering about

so   whenever she wants   to think about
    something that's new

       that she has never
         thought about   before

      she first   has to wait
        until   she has time   to do it

         because it takes
          a   l o n g   time

for her to   sort through
all her pictures

that have already   been stored
inside her head

and to   gather together
the particular pictures   that might

show clues   that pertain
to her   new idea

if   she reduces the   size of the pictures
she can   then handle

up to   eight at one time
placing them in

two rows   of four each
up on that screen   in her mind

but   sometimes
it's counterproductive

to see   all eight pictures   at once
because   with   each one being

shrunk down   so small
it becomes   difficult to see

each picture's   details
which   then can cause

her to lose   the clue
that made

a   particular picture   to be
considered   as an important one

that might help her
in thinking   through

her   new idea   or
in thinking   about

something   to do
that she has never

done before
and is   therefore

something that is
new to her

so   after years   of frustration
        at getting   stuck

        when   she tried to think
                through   new things

        in her head
                and couldn't,

                she   made these steps
                        of what to do

        when thinking about
                a problem,

                        an issue   or
                                some new idea

                and   because these steps
                        work better

                        if they   are not confined
                                to a linear order

                she didn't   number them
                        and then

                                place their numbers   in
                                        an up-and-down column

                        but   instead she drew
                                a circle   inside her head

                                and placed   the steps
                                        around its perimeter

                        so she can enter   at any point
                                trying various ways

                                to solve the dilemma

                                of having

                              no picture   that shows
                                      the current idea

                              or new circumstance
                                      that has   come up

                                      today in her life

so   instead of   linear steps
        she uses   circular rounds   to help her   to solve

              today's   new problems
              or to think about   new ideas

        she starts   moving around   the colors and shapes
              that she uses   to make

                    a picture that shows
                              how her   new idea looks

              and then   this new picture that shows
                    how her idea looks   can take its place

                    because   as a picture it's entitled to
                              its own storage space

              where it can   be stored   permanently
                    for all eternity

                              (like all pictures can be)
                              inside her mind

              and if the occasion   should arise
                    in the future   of her life

                              when she might
                                      choose to share

                    how this picture looks   she can
                              then   retrieve it

                                      from storage
                                      and

                    translate it
                              into words

                    that can be shared
                              with others

                                    94

WAYS TO MAKE NEW PICTURES

DIRECTIONS: pick the point   on the circle perimeter
                    that is the best guess
                          of what will work quickest

        then go   point by point around the circle
                until the new picture
                    has been constructed

(the three most important
      main points
          on the circle perimeter):

POINT   she pulls out   old pictures   that may be   useful
          or   may contain   a possible clue,

            putting them   up on the screen
               eight at   one time

            extracting from each   the useful clues
               bringing these clues

            together   to create
               a new picture

     and if   the new picture   makes sense
        when it's   looked at

            she can know   that it shows
               a new idea

            that is   very likely   a good one
               so   she keeps it

       but   if the picture doesn't look
            quite right

               she knows   that this idea   is probably

                  not very good
            and if that is the case

                 she deletes it

POINT   she looks at   old pictures   one at a time
                to see   if making slight   changes

           in how   it looks
                will render   some picture   that's new

           that will   accurately show
                something pleasant   to see

           and   if it does   she keeps it
                because then   she can know

           the new picture   depicts
                an idea that   is good

    but   if the new picture   looks ugly
           the idea   is a bad one

           and she   deletes it

POINT   she looks   outside her skin
                to see   what is there   that might work

           to make   the new picture
                she wants   to create

           and   whatever looks   useful
                she puts   up on the screen

           until   enough parts   have been saved
                so that she can   start moving them around

           to make   a new picture   that looks
                nice enough   to save

    but   if the pieces of clues   can't make
           a picture that   looks just right

           she can start to delete …
                either all   of the clues

           or just those   she might choose
                to erase   and wait to replace

           with   new clues
                that could be discovered tomorrow

and   maybe then
        one day   if there's a   good reason –

           like   if the picture   seems relevant
               to some   current conversation –

          she could   then translate
               that new picture   from yesterday

                  into   world-people words
                        that the world-people   around her

            might want to hear
                – words that tell about   her idea

                    or her way   to solve some problem
               – words that explain   the way

                  her new picture looks
                      on the screen   in her head

              an example being

                 the words   of this writing
                 that have been written   to show

                    how making new pictures
                    looks to her

CHAPTER THREE

IMPACTS

OF MY

DIFFERENCES

Back Then, when I had launched my new strategy to discover the ways in which I was different from my peers, I imagined that once I had this information, I would simply hide my differences so as to "appear normal," the criteria for discharge from the mental institution. At the time I never realized that once I had discovered my differences, this information would have an emotional impact on me.

Once I had identified my differences, I began noticing not only when my "different-ness" was showing but also the impact of my differences, both on others and on me. I had expected that I would learn about the functional impact of my differences and then figure out how to hide them so that they would come to have no impact on those around me, so that when staff at the institution looked at me, they would see a "normally acting" teenage girl, which I hoped would result in my discharge.

I never expected that this functional exercise would usher forth a personal, emotional, impact. Furthermore, I never expected that I would live in this phase of discovery for several years, even decades, of my life. This phase of my personal journey of discovery saw me through discharge from the mental institution as a teen, and shortly thereafter into postsecondary education and the world of work, followed by volunteerism as a Christian missionary, and a marriage that brought forth three sons – the all-time miraculous blessing of my life.

Come,

      journey with me further

         so together
we might   partake

      of that
         which I discovered

   both the

      functional   impact
         and the

      emotional components
         that my

    different-ness

       creates in
         this world …

People Yardsticks

If

     you measure me

          using your yardstick   of life

             I will not   measure up

                to be   any inches

I'm not the same

     so you can't accurately   measure me

          in the same way

             that you measure

                most   other people

but since nobody   has found

     another way to   measure

        I have come to accept

           that I'll always be   less

             than all of the others

Friends and Acquaintances

for most people   it seems   that
    their friends   are for   a long time –

        usually for   lots of years –
    and having them   is   most definitely   highly rated

for most of   her life it   hasn't been that   way
    and not   because   she wants   no friends

        but just because   Back Then   that's the way   it was
    and 'til recently that's   the way   it has   been

over the years she's noticed   this difference
    and therefore   took particular   interest in watching

        how friends   act when   they are together,
    discovering that   they share   emotions,

        tell their secrets   and sometimes   gossip

all of these things   that friends   share with   each other
    are the very things   she has difficulty   being   a part of

        because of   her

    fundamental   inside
        structural   differences

her insides   are made   in such a way   that
    emotions   aren't   precisely known

        or   readily   available
    as they   seem to be   for   other folks

        but instead   must,   over time,   be discovered
            and processed   and finally   determined

        and even then   aren't always   accurate
            and thus   not something   she is often
                able to share   in the   give-and-take way
            that friends use   to communicate

                in their   current,   ordinary
                    everyday   conversations

she doesn't   have secrets   because
   if it needed   to be said   she has   already said it

     and that is because   whenever   there are
  words   inside her   to say   they create

    a feeling   of pressure   inside her
        that becomes   too painful   if she waits

   so whatever   the words
      happen   to be,   when

     the pressure   is there,

    (to avoid   the pain)
     she just   says them

she sincerely believes   that what she says   is   the right thing
  (because   it's   always the truth   and

    she never   tells stories   or   on purpose   lies)
  she   has to   say these   right words   because

   the build-up   of pressure   inside her
     demands   release

and because she's limited   in the choosing of   WHEN   to say them,
   the words   often are said   at the   wrong time,

    according   to the opinion   of others,
  but   she doesn't   discover   this fact   until later

   when   another person   acts strangely   towards her,
    which becomes   her clue

   that she's   done something wrong   once again
    and now   the chances are

    that   this person

   will never   become
    her friend

for much of her life   she's tried   very hard   to have friends
  (due to   the unspoken   world-rule

   that having friends   is of prime importance),

  but after   the many   repeated instances
    of social blunders   that she's made

but can never   ever   quite figure out
except to   be certain   beyond all   doubt

that   it surely   must,   once again,
be   her own   fault…

Back Then she had   come to   the conclusion
that even though   friends

are so often   so highly rated

it may   be better   for her
to simply enjoy   acquaintances

Back Then she found   that   by doing this
it became   much easier   to accept herself

as a   worthwhile person   living in the world

being just   exactly the way   God made her
accepting   and becoming   comfortable with

handling complications   in life   that often arise
due to   her inside   structural   differences

so, Back Then   instead of trying   so hard
to have friends   and failing

and feeling   defeated and sad
and   unable   to figure it out

or know how   to   ever make
it be   any better …

rather than   always   miserably failing   and losing friends

she learned   to become
comfortably successful   at keeping   acquaintances

and so that she   could still fit in
with   the rest   of the   world-people

around her   she learned
to refer to   her acquaintances

as   friends   even though
she   inside herself   knew

she didn't really   have friends
like everybody else

but probably had
many more acquaintances

and that's   the story   of   friends
     from Back Then

     and   no longer   is   the story
     of   friends from   Now …

once she was   happy with   being herself

     she grew and   matured   and
     came to   know

     the wonder   of   having   a few
     dear friends   of   her own

     – acquaintances who   attached themselves
     to her   soul   and then …

     – she journeyed   the chasm of air
     attaching   her soul   to theirs

     even though   by this   time in
     her life   she is   older –

     later   in years   with
     her children   now grown

People Are Not Interchangeable

sometimes   individual people
    run together

        being   one of   the group
          they are   part of

    which means   she must
        often stop   to think

        before   she speaks

    making certain

        her words are   being spoken
          to the   correct person

sometimes   she is thinking
    so intently   about

        what she has   to say
          that it   doesn't   occur to her

    just then,   at that time,

    that the person
        to whom   she is speaking

    doesn't have   a clue

      as to   what it is
        she is   saying

a long time ago
        she learned   the rule

                that when it comes   to people
                        they   are not   interchangeable

        meaning   that if   PERSON ONE
            has a conversation   with her   today

                … then tomorrow   she can't

        speak her response   to PERSON TWO

            even if   both persons belong
                to the very   same group

sometimes   when she knows
        what she's   talking about

            and the person   to whom   she is speaking

            acts like   he doesn't understand her

        the first thing   she does

            is to repeat herself
                saying her   exact words   over

        but   if   the person
            still acts   confused

            she begins   to wonder …

this may be   one of   those times

        when she needs
            to be talking

                to   PERSON ONE

but because

    both of   them are
       in the same group

it somehow   makes
   perfect sense   to her

    to be talking to   PERSON TWO

but   this kind of mistake   rarely works out

  so   she must   always
      remember   the rule

    that she made for   herself:

"People are NOT interchangeable."

    because   when she   goofs
     and makes this blunder,

it makes   people wonder
   what's wrong   with her

    as she   appears to be
     rather stupid

when   in reality

it's just that at times
   it becomes   rather tiring

for her to

    always keep track
     of all of   the rules

for everything

      each and every   time
          she speaks

the rules of   how to
   say each sentence

      incorporating   their sounds
        of   beginnings and endings

  while choosing   the

     right kinds of
        words to   use

and then
    there are   all of

     the other concerns

of   just how   to conduct
   one's speaking   self

    while in   the company of
      another

remembering …

   time and place,   ·
     volume and sound,

appropriateness of tone,   etc., etc., etc.,

    besides making sure   all of the words
      are directed at   the right person

so please   excuse her
            when she   offends you

                    by taking up
                            your time

    with speaking words

            that are   not
                    even meant for you

        but you can
            be happy

                    knowing   that

as soon   as   you've
        discovered her   error

                    her conversation   with you
                            can   end

        lucky for   you   that you
            are   not her   who

                    (besides being frustrated
                            and now   embarrassed)

        must   now find
            the right person

                    and start   her words
                            all over

many times
        she has   blundered

                    and has   had to
                            start over

some people
    forgive her   and

        some people   don't

every day
    she communicates   with words

      the best that   she can

   with whomever

     the people
        around her   are

no longer
   hiding in   silence

     she now   tries to
       do   her best

  and   just like
     everyone else

      in   the world

  she can't do   any better
    than what her   best is …

    …can you?

How to Be a Non-Alien*

One thing I started doing as a child and still do today, though to a much lesser extent Now than Then, was to make rules for myself whenever I discovered new information. This helped me to fit into the world around me. Once I had made the rule, I could begin to follow it. At first, following a new rule would seem strange, but the more times I followed the rule, the easier it became the next time and the next and the next and the next, again and again.

Repeatedly following a rule internally created the external looks of a path worn in the grass between the homes of two friendly neighbors who often visit each other. And just as it takes walking many times over the same patch of grass to wear it into a path, it takes many times of following the same rule in the same way to put an internal automatic pathway in place.

Sometimes, such as with following my rules of how to be a non-alien, the worn pathway across the grass of my mind was eventually replaced by a cement sidewalk. An internal cement sidewalk might come into being after a particular rule had been manually searched out and activated a multitude of times, so as to have become somewhat automatic.

This, in turn, meant that as long as I wasn't in some way compromised or sensorially overloaded, the correct rule would be automatically activated and applied to a given situation without me having to manually search for it.

I hope people can perhaps now better understand why it is so important for me to follow my own rules in my own way every time there is an occasion to do so. Please keep this in mind as you turn the page and begin reading the five rules, which are but a partial list of the rules from the chapter on speaking from my long ago internally constructed manual called How to Be a Non-Alien.

the realities   of her existence

on this   world-people planet

        tend to   magnify   her differences
                every day
        in numerous ways

                while   she tries   to minimize
                        the impact   her differences
                                will have   upon others –

                because   life is easier
                        for all of them and   for her
                                when   she doesn't   appear

                to be   an alien
                        living in   human skin
                                roaming   around in the earth –

she has a   set of rules
        engineered   specifically   to cause
            her to   look   as if   she belongs

                    in   this world-people   planet
                that others   call home

                    but   to her   feels more
                        like   a place   she is visiting

            while   biding   her time
                    until she can go   wherever the place is
                        where   she might   belong

until then   she lives by   the rules   she created
        designed especially   with world-people   in mind

            people who think   themselves to   be tolerant
                    patient   and kind

            but   nevertheless still
                    have their   limits

                    on   just how much   difference
                they   can handle

                at any   particular time
                        during the day   or night

SOME OF MY RULES FOR HOW TO BE A NON-ALIEN

1.   Use words   that could make   a blind man see
        the picture   in her head

            without using any   more words
        than absolutely   needed

            and   setting a limit
        of two minutes   per picture   in which
            to say them.

2.   Put words   in three groups   to describe
        the three   most important parts
        of her picture.

        (When she got older,
            she discovered
        that each   group of words
            was called   a sentence!)

3.   Remember to stop   and take   a breath
        between each group of words

            because   three groups
        said   all together
        without any   breaks

        cause   world-people   to frown
            and   then not listen.

4.   Besides taking   a breath
        she found   that world-people
            listen   much better

        if each group of words
            has   a beginning

        and   an end   to
            the sound   of them.

5.   Another   thing she discovered
                was the   world-people   order
                        of   topic importance

        like this:

                        #1   people
                        #2   feelings
                        #3   things

        and   in addition to their order

                world-people want   the talking words   of others
        to match their world-people word arithmetic

                like this:

                        People can equal   Feelings.
                        People cannot equal   Things.

                Using world-people   word arithmetic,
                        an example   of how they want   words
                                to be said   would be   like this:

                                It's O.K. to say, "Mom is mad."
                                It's not O.K. to say, "Mom is a volcano."

so   for her   to look   as if she is
        someone   who just   might fit   in the world-people world

                where   she doesn't   belong

        she must use   real words   for speaking
                and put them   in world-people   form

        with these five rules
                being among   the most important

                        for her to follow

                in order   not to be   an alien   on earth
                        who   gets   in trouble.

*From Endow, J. (2006). *Making Lemonade: Hints for Autism's Helpers* (pp. 55-57). Cambridge, WI: Cambridge Book Review Press. Reprinted with permission.

Getting Along in the World

the easiest way
     to get along
         in the   world is to

let things be what they aren't

and

to be what it isn't

you have to
     pay to be loved
         with obedience, etc., etc.

when I knew
     I couldn't
         be loved

because

I couldn't figure out
     what to pay

and

how to
pay it

I only wanted
     to be left
     alone

to gather up
everything

that is me

stuff it inside

and
close the door

I can

    hear

       my differences

in

    the

        breeze

    taking up

      its

         residence

     as it blows

       across

         that soul

      within

        my

          very being

       prompting me

         to close

          the door

       that leads

         inside to

          my soul

        to keep

         the world

          at bay

        that I might

         at least

           stay

         safe inside

          of

           me

the easiest way
        to get along
                in the   world is to

            let things be what they aren't

                and

            to be what it isn't

            (a lie is when they say the words
                    that tell
                            the way it isn't)

so,

        I gathered

            up

        the stuff

            of

                    me

            inside

                my

                        very being

                gently

                    closing

                            the door

                to

                    my

                            soul

                    and putting

a smile

upon my face

I said,

"World,

hello!"

having

learned the

lesson

of just how

one gets along

in the world …

and, the easiest way
to get along
in the   world is to

let things be what they aren't

and

to be what it isn't

Blue-Gray Fringe

living on the fringe

    of humanity

        looking in

           is an alien

                who doesn't belong

                    and is sometimes

                        lonely

sometimes

    wanting to be

        a part of something

           bigger than

                her alien self

                    but simply

                        not knowing how

most of the time

    she's content

        to be an alien

           living on

                the fringe

                    of humanity

but then

    along comes

        a blue-gray

            lonely day

                of wanting

                    more

                        for herself

then clear gray

    sky-water

        slides gently down

      to befriend

        her lonely

            blue-gray

                for the day

Autism's Jail

I've never disobeyed a law,

    but always live in jail.

        Each day the jail bars follow me

            every where I go.

The jail bars are invisible

    yet I can't get past them.

        And even though the door's not locked

        and is always open:

        there seems to be

            no way for me

       to know

          just what to do …

        I see

            the open-standing

              door

      and yet

        cannot

          walk through it.

Whispering Wind

the whisper of   wind

    across my soul

    lets me know

        I'm   different

    sometimes the whisper

        is connected   to

           the stares or   frowns

            of others

sometimes the   whisper

    is connected to

the color of   annoyance

    in another

        when I've   made

          some

           obvious-to-them,

              but not-known-to-me

                (right then   at that time)

                hideous

                  social blunder

the whisper of   wind

across my soul

    lets me know

       I'm   different

     sometimes the whisper

        is connected   to

          the stares or   frowns

            of others

when I try too   hard

to use my words

    and get   stuck

      in their embrace

        speaking   them

          again, again, again and

           again and again and again

            it makes

             the listeners

              eventually become

               altogether

                impatient

sometimes my   words

    are just too   many

       or too   fast

         (or both)

           erupting   like

             popcorn topics

               intruding abruptly

                into the air

                  propelled outward

                    by the pressure

                      felt   within

                        me

and then …

the whisper of   wind

across my soul

    lets me know

      I'm   different

"so if you know,

    why don't you stop?"

      others often wonder

      if I could

I surely would;

indeed,   I'd never start

but I never know

until it's   over

and then

much too   late

to fix

and that's when …

the whisper of   wind

across my soul

lets me know

I'm   different

and   much later

after the fact

I can   connect

the whisper   to

the stares or   frowns

of   others

and always …

the whisper of   wind

across my soul

     lets me know

       I'm   different

Scratched Soul

when you see my   "different-ness"

and point out how   it is amusing

    the sharp edges   of your inner laughter

      make scratches on   my soul

when you see my   "different-ness"

and find it hard   to tolerate

    your annoyance

      makes the scratches   bleed

when you see my   "different-ness"

and cannot stand it   near you

    your disgust

      makes the bleeding   hard to stop

this is why I try   so hard

to only let you know

    my ways of   "sameness"   that match you …

      so I might preserve   my soul

Shadow Living

Shadows of yearning

    of wanting   to belong

      but not always   knowing

        how   to fit in.

                People come and people go,

                  but the Shadows

                      always live   with her.

Walking on tiptoe

    not wanting   to disturb

      the living   humanity

        out there   in the world.

                People come and people go,

                  but the Shadows

                      always live   with her.

Unwittingly   barging in

    where she doesn't   belong

      by blurting   a question

        out of turn.

People come and people go,

but the Shadows

always live   with her.

Appearing uncaring

for lack of   response

when not   clued in

they're   expecting one.

People come and people go,

but the Shadows

always live   with her.

No on-the-spot   words

for when events   change

like a co-worker   leaving

or having   a baby.

People come and people go,

but the Shadows

always live   with her.

Shadows of yearning

    of wanting   to belong

        but not always   knowing

        how   to fit in.

        People come and people go,

        but the Shadows

        always live   with her.

Living with Shadows …

    will it   always be

        or will one day   these Shadows

        fade away

        from me?

        People come and people go,

        but the Shadows

        always live   with her.

(P.S. Remember this poem was written from Back Then. Back Then, for some decades of my life, this was the way things were, but in the time of the Now in my life, it isn't. In the time of Now, the Shadows no longer live with her, perhaps spelling out hope for others' tomorrows.)

Taking Inventory

As an adult woman in a homeless shelter with three small sons, I took inventory. I was in my thirties. All my life I had been very different from people around me. For the most part I had become good at hiding my differences, always trying to find ways to fit in and to "be normal." In my attempts to act normal, at times I was more successful than at other times.

At the age of seventeen, I left the state mental institution for an adult group home for the mentally retarded. I was not yet an adult, but it was the only place that had an opening. At least I got to take a high school chemistry class that I needed to get into a nursing school. I had decided that it would be much better to be a nurse than a patient, so nursing school was the dream I latched onto while institutionalized.

After a few months in the adult care home, a new group home opened up. I was moved to this facility for delinquent teenage girls. It during was my senior year in high school. One of my imposed-by-the-group-home goals was to become more socially like my peers. The other girls took me on as their project, fixing my hair and giving me their clothes to wear so I would fit in better. Then they invited me to go with them to the local hamburger joint, where each Friday evening the group home staff dropped them off around eight o'clock and returned to pick them up at one o'clock the next morning.

It sounded rather boring to me to have to sit in a restaurant for five straight hours, but in order to make progress on my goals I went along. To my surprise, we didn't even sit down at this restaurant! We walked in one door, stopped in the bathroom and left through another door. The rest of the evening was spent going to various bars and discos near the local college. I hated the atmosphere with its smell of smoke, booze and sweat mingled with the unfamiliar sounds and blinking lights.

The girls from the group home instructed me to watch them so that the next week I would know what to do. They gave me drinks and made a big deal of inviting guys to make out with them so that I could see how it was done.

After the first night, I never went out with the girls again. I couldn't handle the sensory assault, and didn't want to add to that "making out" to strangers—whether in the bars or anywhere else! Just from watching, I was sure that I would not like a stranger sticking his tongue in my mouth and his hands in my pants. It seemed utterly ridiculous to have to submit to such behavior just to meet my group home-decreed social goals. I was happy to take the consequences of NOT meeting my goal, which meant that I wasn't in a high enough group level to go out on weekends anyway. (Based on our behavior, and the degree to which we were accomplishing the goals they set for us, we were assigned to various levels that determined certain privileges.) This was perfect; no more worries about having to go out!

After graduating from high school, I got accepted to nursing school and shortly thereafter enrolled and, with the help of my group home staff, moved into the dorm. I got top-of-the-class grades, but was a social failure. Around that time, I had another "nervous breakdown." One day, I simply crawled in bed and stayed there. It felt good to be able to tune out the world. Eventually, I was hauled off to a psych ward, given meds and told that in order to stay in school I would need to see the psychiatrist every two weeks.

Ultimately, I left the nursing program without graduating. I subsequently got a few jobs and places to live, had another psych stay in another town and then met some new friends who "had the Lord." This attracted me because these adults had the rules that Bible-believing Christians have, and they were offering it all to me. I was more than happy to accept. These friends were good people, and I did well for a time. I thought that if I went to Bible School I would do even better, and it felt good to have my friends cheering me on in this venture.

In Bible School, I was again at the top of my class. But again, I ultimately met with failure. When the staff threatened with sending me to a mental institution for some behavior I no longer remember, some friends got me moved to the home of a Christian family in another state. It was the first of a handful of Christian homes I stayed in over the next year or so. It seemed that as long as I had the structure of family life with definite rules and the general quiet atmosphere of Christian living, I got along O.K. I periodically had more "nervous breakdowns," but one thing I liked about the Christians was that they didn't send me off to a mental hospital. They saw the nervous breakdown behavior as problems with demons, and their solution was to pray for my deliverance. At the time, I believed along with them that if the demons could be cast out of my life, I would be just fine – the child of God that I was created to be.

Unfortunately, I never really "got better," but always believed I would, if only I moved somewhere else. This culminated in me moving to a ranch in California called a missionary training center. Once again, I excelled and ended up being on the staff. As in the past, when I had problems, they prayed the demons out of me. At one point, I even came to believe I had been set free of the demons. The only problem was that I had no idea why the demons kept coming back again and again. I was told that I wasn't hanging on to my deliverance, but nobody could tell me what I was supposed to do to keep my deliverance.

Each time I had "demon problems," I was allowed to isolate. But when, after a few days or weeks, someone would remark that I was staying away longer than it would take to recover from the flu or a simple head cold, they got together and prayed the demons out of me. I was then allowed a day or so more in my room, and by then I was usually ready to come out. Looking back, I can see that my sensory system needed down time, and I had figured out a way that worked in that environment to get it.

At the missionary training center, I met my future husband, and the topic of marriage overtook the fact that I kept losing my "deliverance." Everyone focused on me getting married and "knew" that would somehow be the answer to my problems. I married my husband-to-be based on what others were telling me was obedience to the Will of God. I truly wanted to marry this man only because I wanted to be obedient to God and do what I felt God was showing me to do. Everyone around me agreed, including the young man. Thus, we were married, and in a few short years we had three sons.

We stayed as a family at the missionary training center for about seven years, but eventually the marriage was over. I know now that it had not been much of a marriage according to the standards of the world, but more like an agreed-upon arrangement that wasn't bad at the time because we both agreed on being married and the marriage served our needs. I would not do this differently if I had it to do over, because that marriage resulted in my three sons, the biggest blessings and guiding forces of my adult life.

When I left my husband, my children and I moved to a shelter. Since neither my husband nor I had worked for gainful employment, being volunteer missionaries for all of our married life, we had no money. We also had no household goods or furnishings. My children and I had our clothes and some toys and a room in a home-less shelter. It was up to me to forge ahead and make a life for us in the real world. And, so I did. I just kept doing the next best thing I could think to do. As long as I did that, I was fine. If I thought of all the things that might go wrong, then my life got re-ally hard. So I tried to do what I knew worked.

CHAPTER FOUR

LIVING

WITH

AUTISM

During the next years, I got my children settled in school and myself enrolled in college, eventually obtaining a master's degree in social work while simultaneously working in a homeless shelter. During this period, I had another hospitalization with, once again, another diagnosis. This time it was multiple personality disorder and, once again, I "earned" the label by meeting the designated diagnostic criteria. I had therapists along the way who were wonderful people and who believed in me, letting me know they thought highly of me as a person. Looking back, I now know that their caring attitudes towards me were the primary force that healed my soul.

By the time I was in graduate school, I had stopped seeing therapists. I had by then collected several psychiatric labels and had received the corresponding treatments that were in vogue at the time. Even so, in my heart I knew I was the same person I had been as a child. None of the treatments had altered me. I was still a really odd person. The major difference was that now, in my early forties, I knew which aspects of my odd self to hide from others and how to best hide them – at least most of the time.

By the world's standards, I was mostly successful in my day-to-day life. I had a good job and had managed to buy a home in which to raise my then grade-school-aged sons. And again, I found a church, making sure it was one that didn't believe in "deliverance." The people were wonderful; the pastor was lovingly invested in my troubles for quite a long time, but then she left the church and, consequently, was no longer a part of my life. Whenever I experienced troubles. the members of the church offered friendship and caring rather than deliverance. Basically, my life looked pretty ordinary to anyone looking on, but I felt very empty, odd – and always wondered deep down why I wasn't like a real person.

It was likely a good thing that I didn't have much time to devote to thinking about my self-accepted non-human status in the world. One of my sons, who had small problems as a young child, was starting to have bigger problems as he moved into adolescence. He was following a path similar to what mine had been during my preteen and teenage years. He too began stacking up the psychiatric labels and receiving the corresponding treatments and, like his mother, his behaviors and symptoms qualified him for each diagnosis he received. And, like his mother, each treatment failed to bring any lasting relief. He was even placed in the same state mental institution I had been in. Thank God the length of stay had been drastically reduced over the years so instead of him staying for years he was only there for six months.

When he came back home, I became afraid of his ongoing explosive behaviors. Even so, I knew how he felt. I had experienced those same sorts of feelings when I was his age. The difference between us was that I had internalized the feelings and he was externalizing them. It was scary, as he was often violent and sometimes enacted threats on his own life – at other times, on mine. His case worker informed me that my son had already failed all the programs the county had to offer, including a stay at the state mental hospital that had been twice as long as the typical stay. She offered to try to find a foster home placement, but said she didn't know if any home would accept him.

This angered me. My son didn't need a foster home! He had a perfectly good family who wanted him and a mother who understood him and loved him deeply. I was simply running out of options for how to make my home a safe place for all family members, especially since my sometimes violent son was getting bigger and stronger than me.

My anger propelled me to make noise in the right places, advocating for my son and for our family, insisting that the county should be able to provide a teenage child care situation that would keep my son safe while I was at work and offer some respite for my family when his behavior became too extreme to afford safety for others in the home. I was told to call the police when he got violent, but this was not a viable plan unless I wanted my son incarcerated. I didn't. He wasn't a criminal.

Instead, I took time off from work to stay home for a summer in attempts to keep my explosive son safe from himself and out of the grasp of the legal system, while also keeping his brothers safe from his unpredictable outbursts. One morning as my son lay sprawled out on the couch with his head in my lap, he began sobbing and saying, "Mom, I really don't want to be a bad kid." I knew exactly how he felt. I also knew that we had exhausted all treatment options available in the county and in the state. His behaviors were rapidly propelling him out of the mental health system and into the criminal justice system. I feared that if something didn't change pretty quickly, I'd likely be visiting my son in prison one day. His extreme behaviors, even though they were pretty much the same behaviors as always, were now labeled "illegal" due to his age. Temper tantrum behaviors typical of two-year-olds, when acted out in public by a fifteen-year-old, lead to police involvement and legal consequences.

As my son lay sobbing, all I could do was assure him, "I know you are a good kid" and promise him, "We'll figure this out." And then, we did! That very day I started developing a logical and diligent plan for figuring out how to help my son. It culminated in a visual model of four train cars that represented four stages of his escalating behavior, ending with an explosion. The "game" was to figure out how to outsmart the train cars from hooking up because whenever all four cars hooked up, it was never a pretty sight, with the rest of the household becoming victims of a run-away train that exploded in our midst.

During that summer several large tri-fold poster boards stood lined up in our living room as we worked on discovering and implementing strategies that helped prevent my son's behavior from escalating.[1] It was the first time any efforts to remedy the explosive behavior paid off! This was exciting in and of itself, but especially so because I needed to return to work as I had nearly depleted my savings from keeping up with several months of household expenses while having no income.

About that time my son was offered a spot in a new program that allowed him to live at home, attend his neighborhood high school and have supervision after school along with crisis intervention in the home and community twenty-four/seven as needed. In addition, I wanted the staff of the program to use the train model as it was the first thing ever to work with my son and was proving to be extremely helpful. I hauled the poster boards and the case with all the pieces to the program director's office and spent a few hours demonstrating how it worked. I was hired to do staff training, and my son started in this new program.

---

1   I am happy that what began as a almost desperate attempt to help my son has not only benefited him immensely. It is now available commercially to help others – *Outsmarting Explosive Behavior: A Visual System of Support and Intervention for Individuals with Autism Spectrum Disorders* (AAPC, 2009).

After being in this program a short time, my son started seeing a new county psychiatrist. After a few months she diagnosed him with Asperger's Disorder. Then, turning to me, she said, "Now, let's talk about your autism." Aha ... at long last, over the next few months the puzzle pieces of my entire life up to that point began to fit together in a way that made sense! The more I learned and read about autism, the more I understood myself, my son and some of the other children in his new program.

As I had done during my teen years, I began to write poetry to express what was inside me. I felt as if I was in a crash course more intense than any schooling I'd ever known. As I learned to manage my own autism, I shared my newfound knowledge with my son. We made the personal adjustments necessary for the information to be useful and applicable to him.

Within a few years he "graduated" from his program, and I became a staff member, supporting various children with autism spectrum disorders. In time, my son graduated, first from high school and then from a technical college. I moved to a larger city, taking a position as an autism consultant.

During the year immediately before I made this move, I began to discover a lot about the way relationships with other human beings worked for me. Up until then, I had an occasional friend here and there, but those friends eventually always left me as my "differences" got in the way.

I met the first of what I hope ends up to be many real friends. I use the term "real friend" to connotate a person who understands the "real" of me in terms of "the normalcy for one with autism." This person was an author from England who wrote a book about discovering her son's autism and eventually figured out how to help her son by meeting him where he was in his world of autism – joining with him and moving him along in life through shared relationships with various adult mentor playmate friends.

This dear and wonderful woman spent many hours with me on the phone over several months. It was my first experience of unconditional love from someone who understood my autism and didn't allow it to put her off. I will forever be grateful to her, as from that experience I was able to move forward in my life. To meet this lovely woman through the book she authored, read *Autism, The Eighth Colour of the Rainbow* by Florica Stone (Jessica Kingsley Publishers, 2004). One of the gifts she gave me was the encouragement to begin expressing my thoughts to others by sharing my writings. And today, I do just that.[2]

---

2   In addition to this book, I have written *Making Lemonade, Hints for Autism's Helpers* (CBR Press, 2006); *Outsmarting Explosive Behavior; A Visual System of Support and Intervention for Individuals with Autism Spectrum Disorders*; a DVD, *The Power of Words: How We Talk About People with Autism Spectrum Disorders Matters!*; and the *2010 Hidden Curriculum Calendar for Older Adolescents and Adults* – all from the Autism Asperger Publishing Company.

Come again,
take my hand

    walk with me
    through the land

        of learning
        to live

            in the world
            around me

                while my insides
                are now known

                    to be those
                    of a person

                        said to
                    have autism.

World-People Word Amusements

Some world-people wording

    has always seemed a bit odd to her

        and at times the language a bit confusing   for example:

The way she is

        is not   a way of life

        but is   one of life's ways

              she is living out

              simply because she has

                no alternative.

Why did they place her

        in an alternative setting   when she already

        had an alternative setting   placed in her mind?

        Why was it important

           to   put her into   the alternative setting and

           yet   take out of her   that one in her mind?

        Was it so   she could match crazy

        or so   crazy could match her?

When there is a mismatch (or not a good connection)

        between a person   and the outside world

        why is the person   called crazy

        when the person   is normal

          for the way God made her?

And if the person   is not crazy

Then who   is crazy –

          is it God   or the rest of the world?

          No, not God   or the rest of the world

                    (since they are also just the way God made them).

          Maybe nobody's   crazy and

          maybe everybody's   just differently normal?

Why did they say

     she was lost   in   her own world

                    when   her own world was the only place

     she wasn't lost   in?

When the judge made her

     a **ward** of the state   did this mean she

          couldn't move   for**ward**   and she

          couldn't move   back**ward**   but she

          could only   be **ward**?

               And if she stood still so she could be **ward**

               so she wouldn't break the law

                    was she **warding**?

And why then did someone say,

          "Move along, now."   right after the judge

               passed the **warding** law   even though

               they too were   right there and surely

               clearly heard it?

And on the lighter side

    doesn't anyone else

        ever wonder about these kinds of things:

Why is the person who cut off her hair

    called a hair **dresser**   instead of

    a hair **disrober**?

        But then, neither term   makes any   sense

                              since

        hair can neither   put on   or

                      take off   any clothes

                              any way.

      So why not call her

        a hair cutter   (a person who cuts hair)   like

        an ice cutter   (a boat that cuts ice)?

and   if home is where the heart is

        then how can the world have

            homeless people   when

            all people

                have hearts?

and   why do people clearly like to   eat pushups

        but clearly don't like to   do pushups?

           But then if you ask

           if they would rather

eat or do

      they haven't a clue

      as to which one

        to pick for their answer?

and   how is it that

    people can be

      so   sure

      that something is

  so   mind-boggling

      and yet

  so   surely

      can never begin to tell you

        what a boggle is?

Why is it

    that world-people keep on insisting

      (simply by repetitively doing so

    without ever stopping to question)

      that it is their God-given right

        to string words together

        that are utterly nonsensical in meaning

    and then say,   ***"She's resistant."***

    when   she persists

        in not understanding?

Dust Bunny Birdies

I have

    sparkle-dust bunnies

        by the side of my bed

           who live

        in the floor space

           where sunshine

              comes in

                every morning.

Their sparkles

    mingle and float

        in the morning-bright air

        making

      sun-sparkle flecks

        dance with my

          ordinary

              under-bed dust bunnies

        early

            each sun-shiny

              morning.

When

    cleaning day comes

      my dust mop catches

        all

the sun-shiny bunnies

who then

all turn into

dust-baby birdies

when

the dust mop

briskly shakes free

it's

cleaning-caught bunnies

from under

my bed.

The dust-baby birdies

fly into the tree

nesting

until the right time comes.

Then,

a few

birdies each night

find their

way home

to their space

on the floor

by

the side of my bed

and

before you know it

by the end of the

week ...

I have

sparkle-dust bunnies

by the side of my bed

who live

in the floor space

where sunshine

comes in

every morning.

Their sparkles

mingle and float

in the morning-bright air

making

sun-sparkle flecks

dance with my

ordinary

under-bed dust bunnies

early

each sun-shiny

morning!

Ballpark Shorthand

I tend to speak shorthand

    during baseball season

        using ballpark words

           rather than

        taking the time

           to fish for   accuracy

               with

                   my speaking vocabulary.

After all,

    it's summer –

        time to be

           laid back;

      no need   at all
        to pressure myself

            over   speaking,

               is what I reason.

Yesterday

    when it was

        nearly time   to eat

           my son

       walked over

         to

           turn on

             the T.V.

I pointed

      to it   and said,

          "Pizza tornado!"

            which made sense   to him,

        but then …

            he understands

                my summertime

                  ballpark shorthand.

He replied,

      "Pepperoni,

          and you need to say hurricane,

            not tornado,"

        as he turned on

          the TV

            to our favorite

                blue-background news station.

As I turned on

      the oven

          to bake the pizza

            my son

          pointed out to me

            that my summertime

                ballpark speaking shorthand

                  must soon   come to an end.

It's almost time

    for school   to begin

       and he

          reminded me

      that nobody

         outside of   our house

            will understand

               my ballpark words

            (which   to me

             are simply   words

                 that are   close enough

                  to say what   I want …

                like saying tornado

                   when I want   to watch

                     news about   a hurricane's

                    recent destruction).

He also

    dutifully explained

      from his place of teen-aged wisdom

        (which dictates, "Moms are morons.")

     that   I'm not

        ever to   blurt out

          two random words

            strung together

when each

    separate word

      belongs to

        its   own topic

      (like "pizza tornado,"

        for an example)

          whenever his friends

           are visiting us.

My Son Wants More Pets

My son wants a new pet.

    That's ridiculous!

        He doesn't even take care of

           the ones he has!

I say, "Pets need attention,

    exercise, feeding and care.

        You could start by taking care

           of the pets that you already have."

"I don't have any pets,"

    my son replied.

        "Why do you say so?

           You're telling a lie!"

No, it's true –

    just look outside!

        We have worms in the garden

           and ants in the driveway;

               bees on the flowers

               and birds in the trees

                    the squirrels run right up the feeder

                  and eat all the birdseed

                    while the crickets screech

when we try to sleep

and, of course,

there are mosquitoes galore

all over the place.

"Oh mom. Get real!" he says, rolling his eyes.

Well then, come on inside

and all the more pets you will see!

(The inside pets all belong to my son,

but he hasn't yet taken care of them.)

I'm sure in your sneakers

there lives a pet,

but probably dead

from the smell of it.

I'm certain by now

there are live organisms

in your damp-waded

beach towel

left over from

last week's swimming

and stuffed into the black hole

of under-your-bed-forgotten.

And while you are down there

     looking under your bed

          you will find more pets than you'll need

               for the rest of your life.

See all those dust bunnies

     that keep multiplying?

          You'll never run out;

               they'll keep you stocked!

So, my dear son

     you must start to take care of

          these numerous pets that you have

               before we can talk about getting more.

"Oh, mom. Get real!" he replies, rolling his eyes.

As a mom with three teenaged sons, my life was busy. Knowing I had autism was a relief. Often when I needed to figure out something in life, I would write a poem. It helped when I could use my literal and concrete way of understanding the world to write about my everyday experiences of life.

I also used my neurology to look at my insides and write about what I saw. This allowed me to look at the sound and movement of my inside colors and translate them into words that could be written on paper. These paper words became my way of managing emotions and dealing with sensory overload in the literal, concrete, think-in-picture style that made sense to me.

From this place of how I am able to understand myself, I invite you to read the next section of poems. No More Room in My Suitcase, I Am Queen and Fairy Tale Updates are all examples of how I use poetry to translate the color pictures inside me into words that can help me discover and outsmart my everyday sensory overload and often elusive grasp on managing emotions.

No More Room in My Suitcase

there's no more room
in the suitcase

I use

to travel through
today

no place to put
any more wondering about

what

I still need to somehow
get figured out

so what you see
when you look at me

for the rest of the day

will truly be
what you get

'cuz in my suitcase
I can't fit

any more info today …

I'm already on
overload—stuck and …

no matter how much
you'd like

or I'd want

it just isn't
going to happen

I can't act
          any differently

               than

                    what you
                         can see

when my suitcase
          gets full

               before

                    the day's living
                         is done

is when
          I try to hide

               from

                    all of the world
                         outside me

I go for a walk
          with my suitcase stuffed full

               and throw

                    all my cares
                         to the wind

there's room in the wind
          for all of life's leftovers

                    that can't fit into
                    my suitcase
                         anymore today

so if at the end of the day
        I behave in a way

                that you don't

                        much like
                                (and maybe you do this, too)

my advice to you
        is to do what I do

                when my suitcase is full:

                        Toss
                                whatever is left to the wind

and know that tomorrow
        we'll start the day new

                with our suitcases

                        for life
                                nearly empty …

but even though I explain this
        so plainly

                I also do know

                        it won't work for most folks
                        in the world

some can't comprehend
        only one suitcase

                for

                        each day
                                of life's travels

so how can I
      expect forgiveness

         when

            my end-of-the-day
               behavior unravels?

I can't
      so I don't

         but even so want you to know

            that I'm not
               an entirely ugly-bad person

if you can't comprehend me
      and I can't change my ways

         might we …

            just might we
               agree? …

maybe we both
      could agree

        it's O.K.

           that we don't always
             understand each other

we could then
      still be friends

        for most of the day
         before my suitcase

           becomes overloaded

I Am Queen!

In my dream

    I am queen

        of all the air around me;

    in charge of words

        and of their sound

            I gather tools around me.

When too many words

    pollute the air

        I grab my broom to sweep them

    or else turn on

        the vacuum's whoosh-suck

            to delete them!

When ugly words

    pollute the air

        with their smoky haze

    I grab the Windex

        and a rag:

            spray and rub away.

When hurting words

    pollute the air

        I run for the garden hose;

    direct the stream

        to shoot them down

            before they make gray-woes.

When words aren't right

    and thus pollute

        I fix the mess they make.

    I keep air clean

        from word debris;

            that's me: Air-janitor word-police!

But in reality

    I am queen

        of air and all words in it;

    in charge of words

        and of their sound

            I reign o'er Clean Air Kingdom!

Fairy Tale Updates

… a knight in shining armor

    to rescue

        the damsel in distress.

… a beautiful princess

    to kiss

        the frog into a prince.

        Fairy tales abound galore

          but in real life

            I see

          damsels coping

            on their own,

              living resiliently

            while all the frogs

              croakingly boast

                of their handsom – nimity!

CHAPTER FIVE

EMBRACING

LIFE

AUTISTICLY

As far back as I can remember, I knew I was "different." Over the years, a smorgasbord of psychiatric labels have been used to describe my differences. At the time of this writing, I have been living with my autism label for nearly a decade. I now understand that it is highly unlikely I ever really had any of the mental illnesses that were attributed to me. Instead, I have had since birth what is now known by the medical profession as a neurologically based disorder of the brain called autism.

I thought that after so many years, there was nothing as wonderful as getting a label that finally fit! I immediately became a sponge, absorbing information about autism, reading everything I could. I was glad to have kept much of my poetry from the years before I received the autism diagnosis, as the poems accurately reflect so many aspects of autistic life. At the time I penned the poems, I wrote about what was inside me as a way to try to understand myself and my experience in and of the world around me. Little did I know these poems would ever hold any interest to anyone other than me.

It was extremely liberating to finally be able to understand the movies in my head as an autistic style of thinking rather than a mental illness, a nervous breakdown or being possessed by demons. And now that much of my yester-years have been sorted out, I have become aware of the privilege of being able to move into the future of my life. For so many years until receiving my autism label, during times in my life when my differences would show, I always looked towards that day in the future when I would no longer have the so-called mental or demonic problems. Now I know better. Now IS that future!

So,   come along
        once again

                and travel with me
                        as walking
                        hand in   hand

                together we
                        survey   this
                        new road

                                called Today

                        as I begin
                                to embrace
                                my autism

                                loving the
                                        "real" of me

                                just as I am …

                                        learning to live
                                        comfortably with

                                                the autism of me
                                                in my Now

No Druthers

If she had

her druthers,

would she

rather be

a part of

world commonality?

Not really.

She's content

in being

who she is

inside

her own skin,

walking around

in the world

outside her,

often bumping up

against differences

causing her

to sift for sameness

to make a match

with the insides

of another,

knowing that

at least one

universal difference

for each person

is known –

accounting

for individuality

in that world-sea sameness

to which

we all

cling to

for life

while supporting

diversity's greatness,

but secretly

not wanting

to be

any different

from others.

What a mind-boggling

dichotomy!

Regardless of

who we are

or

how our being

has been formed,

it's only when

we are able

to embrace

this dichotomy's

two sides

rather than

choosing

one or the other

that we can

truly

live with

ourselves

inside our

world-people planet

feeling

mostly comfortable

with our

own insides

and outsides

and with

one another.

Eventually when my children were grown, I made the move to a new city, a new job and new opportunities to not only give, but to receive, love from other human beings. This changed my perspective on life. Today I have a handful of wonderful true friends, among them my best friend, Kate. I first met Kate through reading a book she co-authored called *Walk Awhile in My Autism* (CBR Press, 2005).

The most phenomenal blessing Kate has brought to my life is her belief in the good of me. Kate believes in me – completely and without reserve. Because of Kate's total acceptance of me as a wonderfully unflawed human being whom she hoped would one day become her friend, I was set free.

What an unspeakable relief to finally, after all these years, come into the knowledge that I am an O.K. human being just the way I am! Because Kate believed in me and accepted me just as I was, it paved the way for me to start accepting myself.

Today, I no longer think of myself as "having autism." My response to the idea of having autism, as in having a disorder or a disease, has metamorphosed over time. At first, I was thrilled to finally be given an appropriate label because it brought some sense to my life wrought with differences. Later I became disgruntled, and eventually downright angry, at the assumption that I had some sort of disorder that needed to be fixed, or worse yet, a disease that needed to be cured. I knew that I was born autistic. It is who I am.

I was not born as a world-person with typical neurology who had somehow acquired a disorder or a disease called autism. Instead, I was already autistic when I was born, just as I was already blue-eyed and female. My female gender, blue eye color and autistic neurology are part of what defines who I am.

Just as my female gender and blue eye color were not added after my birth, neither was my autism. Therefore, I am autistic; I am blue-eyed; I am female. I am an autistic blue-eyed female. My autistic neurology does not need to be fixed or cured any more than my blue eye color or my female gender needs to be fixed or cured.

Today, research is showing the genetics of autism. I am hoping that one day the so-called "treatment" for autism will be called "support" and that we will come to allow autistic people to be who they are, providing them with the support they choose to enable them to live comfortably in the world around them.

Even though I am inherently perfect just as I am (just as God created me) I often choose to learn how to become more comfortable in my body, which in turn allows me to be more comfortable in the world around me. The long-ago discoveries I made about my inside wiring and my collection of little stones that represent the WHO, the HOW and the WHAT of me now make complete sense.

Today I accept the WHO, the HOW and the WHAT of me as the way I am, an intrinsically good creation! Indeed, these days I am becoming quite comfortable with the person of me inside my skin –

the real of me

just as I am

perfect and
complete

and incredibly free –

free to be

the WHO
the HOW
  and
the WHAT   of me

with Paper Words
now telling my story –

    today
    being comfortable

        inside
        my own skin

            no longer
            needing to hide

                any autistic
                neurology …

                    AND

                in charge of
                choosing

                    when and where
                    to copy

                    the ways
                    of the world

                    to maximize
                    personal efficiency

Time, A Precious Commodity

Time is a precious   commodity
      and some say I   take up too   much of it …

… It takes Time for   words
    – to ferret out the   important ones
        from all the   rest of the   hullabaloo

    – to brace and   wait for   the piercing pokes
      they make on my inside parts to   stop

        Time …
          so I might   begin to listen to   the sound of   them
           to   sort them   out
           and decipher them for   meaning.

        Time …
        incoming words take Time …

Time is a precious   commodity
      and some say I   take up too   much of it …

… it takes Time for   changing my   thoughts

    – from this   topic to   another

    – from being   with my   words
      to then being   with   yours
and back   and forth   again   and again

    Time …
      processing words takes   Time

Time is a precious   commodity
          and some say I   take up too   much of it …

          It's hard to   listen faster
                    process   more quickly
                         or share my   inner self with you

                    when I don't   have
                         a way to   "go"

                    when your   commodity of   Time
                         says   "now" …

                    … and this is why I don't.

Words, the Currency of Time
(Directions for How to Spend Non-Cents Dollars)

"Spend your Time wisely,"

    is a   saying   I've heard.

The currency of   this Time

    I've learned

        is to   use One's   words.

    If One uses   words   galore

        One might   captivate   Another …

        … sometimes a   bittersweet   victory   to gain

        a Time-limited   captive

        who   hears the   words

        that   bury my   soul …

… as I spend

this   currency of   words

        for   Time,

        however   unwisely,

                    offering dollars

                    devoid

                        of cents,

                    the   gold of my soul

                        remains

                            unspent.

    Today, my handful of friends have time for the "real" of me. I find it strange that many people think they have a more meaningful relationship with me than they do, especially when they rarely have time to spend with me. I have no idea where they get this idea, but I guess it is a good problem to have because it is better to have people thinking they are my close friends than to have enemies.

    One thing all my very close friends have in common is that, besides having time for me, they allow me to be their friend. Most people who imagine themselves to be my friend are very kind and giving people and like to be known for being helpful to me, an autistic person, but they do not ever make the space for me to be their friend back. Thus, it is not a true friendship because they do not find me to be necessary to the core of their being.

    My closest friends and I have reciprocal relationships. Both of us find the other necessary in our lives in a way that is not demanding. I find Kate necessary, because when I am with Kate I can be my very best – the person I was created to be. Sometimes this looks great and at other times it looks really messy. But no matter how it looks, I am able to be who I am and it is O,K.

    Kate has similar feelings. She says that I bring out the best in her. Sometimes that looks good and sometimes it doesn't. We know each other's faults and flaws and can love each other through them. This means that our faults and flaws don't become each other's pet peeves. We both are limited and imperfect and are O.K. with that in ourselves and in each other.

    This is how it is with my closest friends. We find each other necessary and care deeply for one other. When I'm allowed to show my caring however I want, I am able to freely spend the gold of my soul, often with abandon, on my friends. I love it and would not live my life any differently. The meaningfulness of life for me, an autistic, is in the reciprocal relationships of my everyday life. So, all in all, when it comes to the truly important stuff of life, I am more like you than autism can ever make me different. Imagine that!

To Whom It May Concern

It is   often said

      that   autistic people

         lack feeling

    and therefore

         cannot show

            much   caring

               towards   another.

People   who

      write this

         in books

    or   say this

        when   speaking

           obviously   are not   autistic

        because

           if they   were

               they would   know

                  this fact:

Caring

      is   perceived differently

         and

    if allowed

        by others

           can be   shown –

        although,

           perhaps

               in

           a different   way

than

most people

might show   it.

P.S.

Is

it

necessary

to refer   to

my different   ways

as   "odd?"

When

you do so

it   is not

only   hurtful,

but also

speaks

of   your own

limitations

and   narrow boundaries.

So, please –

in order

that   we both

may become

better   people,

will you   stop?

Just Wondering,

Judy

SHARING OUR WORLDS

At the time of this writing, the latest statistics report that 1 in 150 children in the United States have autism or a closely related disorder (reported by the Centers for Disease Control, Feb. 8, 2007). The following poem was my initial response to hearing this information.

United Living

It's a big   world out there
      plenty of room for us all

            whether we are part of
                  the one hundred   forty-nine strong
            or the single entity   labeled "autism"
                  standing alone –

            Each one of   us is given
                  a place in the   world
            our very own spot
                  to grow   into

      For many years in my   spot
            there were   shadows

                  Shadows of yearning
                        of wanting   to belong
                              but not always   knowing
                              how   to fit in.

                  Unlocking mysteries
                        being   comfortable in
                              the body I was sent to earth
                              to live my life from.

                  A self-imposed mission
                        years spent in   unraveling
                              strategies for   dispelling
                                    multiple-shadow   mysteries.

                  Now able to share
                        from my place in the world
                              relaying discoveries
                                    some musings and   wonderings.

      And yes, it's a big   world out there
            plenty of room for us all

whether we are part of
        the one hundred   forty-nine strong
or the single entity   labeled "autism"
        standing alone –

Each one of   us is given
        a place in the   world
our very own spot
        to grow   into

Many years in my   spot
        there were   shadows

            Then, my shadows of   autism
                became manageable in
                    the world at   large .
                        outside of my skin.

        A world of
            one hundred fifty   united
                where each one
                    "as is" can   belong.

        No longer a need
            to separate autism   out
                for practical   living
                    into one hundred forty-nine and   one.

Scratched Soul Sequel

when you see my   "different-ness"

    and wonder how   it will impact our relationship

        your willingness to   connect with me

          paints calmness on my soul

when you see my   "different-ness"

    and respond to   my challenges with kindness

        assuming I'm doing my best in the moment

          your caring sets free my   heart-felt reciprocity

when you see my   "different-ness"

    and yet can look beyond   and come to know

      the inner real   of me

         the sound of our colors dancing   make my spirit whole

and this is how   I come to understand

    I have a human place   on earth

        knowing that I am but one   of two

         individual   matching human souls

         choosing to walk   together

          in this   temporal space

            that now   can be called

            "our world"

Books and Materials by Judy Endow

**Outsmarting Explosive Behavior
– A Visual System of Support and
Intervention for Individuals with
Autism Spectrum Disorders**
(package includes poster-size visual, facilitator handbook and student workbook)

Code: 9035
Price: $49.95

**Paper Words, Discovering and
Living with My Autism**

Code: 9036
Price: $18.95

**The Power of Words: How We
Talk About People with Autism
Spectrum Disorders Matters!** (DVD)

Code: 9730
Price: $9.95

**Making Lemonade, Hints for
Autism's Helpers**

Code: M125
Price: $20.00

APC

Autism Asperger Publishing Company
P.O. Box 23173
Shawnee Mission, Kansas 66283-0173
877-277-8254
www.asperger.net